MAKE
THE
CONNECTION

LINKING BIBLICAL TRUTHS
FOR TRIUMPHANT LIVING

DR. JAMES F. ENGLE

Green Tree Press
Fort Lauderdale, FL

Cover Design by Hannah Sorensen, Tammy Hughes and Tom Hughes.

Published in Fort Lauderdale, Florida by GreenTree Press.

ISBN: 978-0-9828721-3-0

Printed in the United States of America

To Sue...

…my favorite person…bringing joy to my life…
…my life partner…bringing stability to my life…
…my staunchest supporter…bringing encouragement to my life…
…my kindest critic…bringing quality to my life…
…my best friend…bringing companionship to my life…

ACKNOWLEDGEMENTS

L earning curves are always challenging. Learning curves are also a great time to rely on others for help, consultation and assistance. This initial venture into authoring and publishing a book has been a rewarding and demanding experience.

This project would not have been completed without a great team of people, each member of the team being there at just the right time with just the right assistance. Sue Engle heads the list for her support of the idea and encouragement throughout the project. Tammy Hughes sat at her computer, patiently working on revision after revision. Sara Anderson, Cindy Baumgardner, Loren Eaton, Matt Hoffland, Kathy McEvoy, Jan Weisser, Diane Windle and Kris Zeidler joined the proofreading team.

The staff at GreenTree Press went the extra mile. John Sorensen walked with me through the entire publishing process, providing valuable counsel and insight. Hannah Sorensen took the final manuscript, preparing it for publication. To each of the above people I publicly express my gratitude. This group brought a variety of talents, abilities and perspectives together for a common goal.

All of the people mentioned above have one very important thing in common. We all have trusted Jesus Christ as Savior and are seeking to live obediently under His Lordship. That is the sole purpose of this book.

To this end this book is dedicated.

INTRODUCTION

And we know that for those who love God all things work together for good, for those who are called according to His purpose.

Romans 8:28

During my three-and-a-half decades of pastoral labor, I have become increasingly cognizant of our tendency to separate and segment our lives into small, isolated pockets. When this happens, an unfortunate, and even dangerous, disconnect occurs between our Lord Jesus Christ and the various dimensions of everyday living.

We must not remove any part of our lives from the domain of Christ and the oversight of His Word. God's providence and sovereignty over all things, as indicated in Romans 8:28 above, is linked to the promise that He works all things for our good and His glory. God connects what we tend to disconnect.

This volume is dedicated to seeking out, amplifying and applying the connections that the Lord makes as He holds and works all things together for our good and His glory. Each chapter highlights one of these connections. To coin a phrase, I am calling them "doctrinal devotionals."

You may find some of these connections logical and obvious. I have included them because, although logical and obvious, they are often ignored. They deal with the very basics of living with Christ as Lord.

Other connections only become apparent as one's biblical knowledge and understanding deepen. These need to take root in our lives as spiritual growth takes place. Daily, regular and disciplined time invested into the Word of God brings about that continued work of the Spirit in conforming us to the image of Christ.

Still other connections, on the surface, appear to be contradictions. They are not. They are clear expressions of the radical nature of the Gospel and its implications for our lives. These challenge the areas where our fallen nature and our increasingly godless culture seek to press us into its mold. Abraham Kuyper wrote, "In the total expanse of human life there is not a single square inch over which Christ, who alone is sovereign, does not declare, 'That is Mine!'"

We all have territory in our lives that we are attempting to own and control. It is my prayer that the Lord will use these doctrinal devotionals to lead us to relinquish those territories to the control of our Lord. After all, the territory really is already His.

TABLE OF CONTENTS

CONNECTING

Sin & Salvation

A ssumption is the lowest form of knowledge. People do it all the time to their detriment. I will pick on my world for an illustration. My world is the local church, where my role is the preaching/teaching pastor. Many people who are members of the church I pastor assume that if a person visits our church, they already are followers of Christ.

It would be easy to assume that anyone who picks up a Bible-based book like this one already understands the Gospel and has become a follower of Christ. I am not going to make that assumption.

All of the other connections considered in this volume are academic and meaningless without comprehending the connection between sin and salvation. Comprehension, in this instance, means understanding, experiencing and applying this biblical truth to your personal life.

What follows is not my opinion or my personal interpretation. It is the plain and clear teaching of the Bible. To get right to the heart of the matter, I pose two questions:

QUESTION #1

Are you 100% sure that if you died today you would go to heaven?

The Bible states that we can know, for certain, that we will go to heaven when we die. We can have a "know-so" faith in a "hope-so" world.

> *I write these things to you who believe in the name of the Son of God **that you may know that you have eternal life**.[1]*

QUESTION #2

Suppose you were to die today and stand before God, and He were to ask you, "Why should I let you into My heaven?" What would you say?

According to the Bible, there is only one way to answer this question.

GRACE

Heaven, eternal life, living forever in God's presence, is a free gift. As a gift, it is not earned or deserved. Also, it is not something that can be paid for or purchased. Consider these two biblical statements:

> *For the wages of sin is death, but the free gift of God is eternal life in Christ Jesus our Lord.[2]*

> *For by grace you have been saved through faith. And this is not your own doing; it is the gift of God, not a result of works, so that no one may boast.[3]*

---

[1] 1 John 5:13 (emphasis added).

[2] Romans 6:23.

[3] Ephesians 2:8-9

MAN

We are all sinners. Therefore, we cannot save ourselves.

Sin separates us from an all-holy and perfect God. Sin is much more than the "big things" like murder, robbery and adultery. Sin is not limited to actions. Sin can be an attitude, a thought, a word. Sin can be not doing something that we should have done. Here is a good one sentence definition of sin: Anything that falls short of God's perfect standard.

...for all have sinned and fall short of the glory of God...[4]

Let me illustrate that our sin is far more serious than we realize or even want to admit. With the thousands of thoughts, thousands of words and thousands of actions that take place in a single day in each of our lives, I wonder how many times we fall short of God's perfect standard. One hundred...fifty... twenty-five?

For our illustration, we will be exceptionally good people and only have three sins on our list. In reality, the number is much higher. Yet, even at our three sins a day, in a year's time that adds up to well over a thousand. With the average age now in the 70's, even with this conservative estimate, we will amass a record of more than 70,000 times that we fell short of God's perfect standard. Can you imagine walking into a traffic court with 70,000 speeding tickets and declaring to the judge that you are a really good driver? Ludicrous!

---

4 Romans 3:23

We are not pretty good people, we are serious sinners. As mentioned earlier, the wages of sin is death. People often state that they only want God to be fair. To be fair is to give what is deserved.

You and I are sinners. So, if God was fair and simply gave us the wages we have earned, we would be dead. In fact, that is what we are as sinners—spiritually dead.

GOD

God is merciful and does not want to punish us. But God is also just and must punish sin. Two short verses validate these vitally important dimensions of God's character.

God is love.[5]

[He] will by no means clear the guilty...[6]

What has been said thus far presents us with a problem, a serious problem, a problem we cannot solve for ourselves. The Good News is that God solved our problem in the person of Jesus Christ!

JESUS CHRIST

Here is where the Person and Work of Jesus Christ are essential. Jesus is God, born into this world as a man. This is called the incarnation and is celebrated each Christmas. The first verses of John's Gospel emphasize this truth:

---

[5] 1 John 4:8b

[6] Exodus 34:7b

In the beginning was the Word, and the Word was with God, and the Word was God. And the Word became flesh and dwelt among us, and we have seen His glory, glory as of the only Son from the Father, full of grace and truth.[7]

You will notice that "Word" is capitalized. This is because it is a name, or a title, for Jesus. So, this verse could be read: In the beginning was Jesus, and Jesus was with God and Jesus was God. Jesus became flesh and made His dwelling among us.

While Jesus accomplished so much in His brief time on this earth, there is one accomplishment that stands head and shoulders above all the rest. Jesus died on the cross to pay the penalty for our sins and rose again from the dead to prove He had purchased a place in heaven for us.

The last sentence Jesus spoke from the cross before breathing His last breath was, "It is finished!" Actually, in the language He used, it is a single word that could be translated "paid in full." Having lived a sinless life, He paid the sin debt of every person who trusts in Him for forgiveness.

All we like sheep have gone astray; we have turned—every one—to his own way; and the LORD has laid on Him (Jesus) the iniquity of us all.[8]

For our sake He made Him (Jesus) to be sin who knew no sin, so that in Him we might become the righteousness of God.[9]

---

[7] John 1:1,14.

[8] Isaiah 53:6.

[9] 2 Corinthians 5:21.

Having perfectly satisfied the righteous requirements of God's holy law, Jesus died as our substitute, in our place. This is the ultimate expression of the holy love and holy justice of God.

> *...but God shows His love for us in that while we were still sinners, Christ died for us. Since, therefore, we have now been justified by His blood, much more shall we be saved by Him from the wrath of God.*[10]

The wages for sin now having been paid, we can become the recipients of the gift of eternal life.

FAITH

This gift—the gift of eternal life—is received by faith. Saving faith is not simply head knowledge. I can know facts about Jesus, such as I might know facts about George Washington and Abraham Lincoln. Knowing about someone and having faith in that person are very different matters.

Saving faith is not temporary faith. When a loved one gets sick, we might pray for him. That is health faith. When we fly in an airplane to go on vacation, we might pray for safety. That is traveling faith. These are temporary matters; when the loved one is no longer sick or the trip is over, we don't need that faith any longer.

Saving faith is trusting in Jesus Christ alone for your salvation. It is trusting what He did on the cross to pay for your sins.

---

[10] Romans 5:8-9.

When you trust Christ, you stop trusting in your own supposed goodness, or religiosity, or any long list of good deeds.

The apostle Paul is the most famous missionary in the history of the Christian church. While imprisoned in the city of Philippi, he had a dramatic encounter with the Roman jailer who was working the third shift. You can read the account in Acts 16:25-40. Shortly after midnight and following a great earthquake, the jailer posed a profound question to Paul, who responded with an even more profound answer.

> *And the jailer called for lights and rushed in, and trembling with fear he fell down before Paul and Silas. Then he brought them out and said, "Sirs, what must I do to be saved?" And they said, "Believe in the Lord Jesus, and you will be saved.*[11]

Remember, your only contribution to your salvation is your sin. It is your sin, which separates you from God, that makes your salvation through the work of Christ necessary.

A helpful illustration will give you a visual as to how this must apply to you and your life. In your mind I want you to see the two of us sitting in chairs around your kitchen table. At the side of the table next to me is an empty kitchen chair. To illustrate saving faith, I will pose three questions regarding that empty chair. First, do you believe that chair exists? Is it real? The obvious answer is yes. Next, do you believe that the empty chair would hold me if I sat in it? Again you would answer in the affirmative.

---

[11] Acts 16:29-31.

Finally, why isn't that empty chair holding me up right now? Because I am not sitting in that empty chair.

Now, we are going to label our three chairs. The chair in which you are sitting has a label bearing your name. The chair on which I am sitting is labeled the "Jim" chair. The empty chair is labeled the "Jesus" chair.

All of us are born sitting in the chair bearing our name. Sinners though we are, we come to the conclusion that God should let us into heaven because we are basically good people, trying our best, not intentionally harming anyone. We are sitting on the chair of our good works.

So, if we had to provide an answer as to why God should let us into heaven, we would respond, "I should get in because I am a good person, trying my best and not intentionally harming anyone."

If you or I answered that way, we would enter a Christless eternity in hell. This is exactly what we deserve.

To receive the gift of eternal life, we must get up from the chair bearing our name and sit down in the Jesus chair. We transfer our trust from ourselves to Jesus Christ alone for our salvation.

The question to you at this point is simple and straightforward. Are you sitting in the chair bearing your name? If you are, it is time for you to confess your sin, acknowledge that you deserve to go to hell, thank God for sending Christ to die on the cross for your sin and receive Christ as your Savior and Lord.

But to all who did receive Him (Jesus), who believed in His Name, He gave the right to become children of God, who were born, not of blood nor of the will of the flesh nor of the will of man, but of God.[12]

Christ as Savior calls you to agree that you are a sinner and Christ is the only Savior.

Christ as Lord calls you to repent (which means to make a behavioral U-turn), agreeing that your way is the wrong way and that Christ's way is the right way. It means that you get down off of the throne in your heart and let Jesus take His rightful place on that throne.

Now a word to the second group reading this chapter. If you are already in the Jesus chair, if you have trusted in Jesus Christ alone for your salvation, pause right now and express afresh to the Lord your gratitude for your salvation and renew your commitment to live with Him as your Lord.

The pages that follow are for both the brand new Christian and the person who has known Christ for decades. If this volume can assist you in growing in your walk with Christ and deepening your serious discipleship as His follower, it will have fulfilled its purpose.

---

[12] John 1:12-13.

CONNECTING

Abiding & Abounding

[Jesus said], "I am the true vine, and my Father is the vinedresser. Abide in Me, and I in you. As the branch cannot bear fruit by itself, unless it abides in the vine, neither can you, unless you abide in me. Whoever abides in Me and I in him, he it is that bears much fruit, for apart from Me you can do nothing."
John 15:1,4,5

And God is able to make all grace abound to you, so that having all sufficiency in all things at all times, you may abound in every good work.
2 Corinthians 9:8

O ne of the marvelous blessings of God's grace is the "much more" that it makes available to us. We come to the cross empty handed—"nothing in my hands I bring, only to the cross I cling!"—and there experience salvation as a gift of God's grace. At that moment of our conversion, the Lord makes available to us the treasures of His eternal storehouse. Yet, while God is generous, He is not wasteful.

If we think we can grab what we want from Him and run to fulfill our own desires and agendas, we are sadly mistaken. In the vinedresser/vine-and-branches snapshot, it is clear that such an option is not available. As usual, all of this is accomplished and achieved on God's terms, not ours.

This is where the connection is established between abiding and abounding. Read these verses again, slowly and carefully, asking the Spirit to grant you the wisdom to learn what you need to learn from the very mind of God.

Abiding is an intriguing word and an even more intriguing spiritual reality. First, it prioritizes relationship. Salvation restores a relationship that was severed by sin. Sin separates. When the act of saving faith took place, this relationship was restored. In the imagery of John 15, that is when our heavenly Father, the Vinedresser grafted us into Jesus, the Vine. This relationship is personal and permanent.

Next, it promotes intimacy. A branch cannot be connected to two vines. Our intimacy with Jesus is exclusive and not to be shared. Also, this closeness cannot be transferred. A branch cannot leave one vine to move to another. This is a practical application of the First Commandment, "You shall have no other gods before Me" (Exodus 20:3).

Thirdly, it personalizes the connection. This connection is with a living Person. Jesus is the Vine. You and I, redeemed people, have our personal, individual lives grafted into the Person of Jesus Christ. How magnificent it is that Jesus provides personal care and guidance in each of our lives!

Fourthly, it pictures dependence. Without the vine, the branches not only are useless, they do not even exist. The branches depend on the vine for sustenance, nutrition—everything.

Finally, it points to the purpose of why branches exist. Bearing fruit is the sole purpose, not to grow bigger and bigger or have a lot of leaves. Also, branches do not produce fruit, they bear fruit. Pruning increases fruitfulness, and that is the business of our Vinedresser in His work with the branches.

Our Vinedresser does not want to hear people walking by His vineyard remarking, "My, what large vines. My, what beautiful vines." The only useful compliment is, "What fruitful vines!"

To these ends, our Vinedresser engages in the pruning process on us, the branches grafted into the Vine.

> [Jesus said], "Every branch in Me that does bear fruit He lifts up, and every branch that bears fruit, He prunes, that it may bear more fruit."[13]

While on a ministry trip to Fresno, California, I once visited a vineyard owned by a member of the church. I saw some vines that had just been pruned and some that were soon to be pruned. I was amazed at the difference. That visual illustrated to me just how much the vinedresser had cut away. The purpose was to increase fruit bearing.

If you were to be painfully, even brutally, honest with yourself, you could identify some attitudes, actions and/or habits that need pruning in your life. By the way, if you cannot identify anything at all, that is exactly what needs to be pruned. If you need a label, try pride or blind-spot. Pride contends that, "I am okay just the way I am. I have arrived. I have achieved." No, you haven't.

Any pruning that needs to be done has one goal: that your abiding may abound in the work of the Lord in your life. Thus, Jesus focuses the analogy on the nature of a vine, building

---

[13] John 15:2 (author's translation).

words of encouragement as He prunes His disciples unto greater fruitfulness.

Consider the progression of fruitfulness in this John 15 passage. Let me state the principle before pointing out this progression: No matter how fruitful you are at this stage in your spiritual life, the Lord has purposed that you become even more fruitful in the future. This prohibits retiring or coasting, spiritually speaking. Now, the progression:

- Verse 2 – every branch that does not bear fruit...
- Verse 2 – every branch that bears fruit...
- Verse 2 – that it (the branch) may bear more fruit...
- Verse 8 – that you bear much fruit...
- Verse 16 – that you should go and bear fruit and that your fruit should abide...

Pruning is an activity of God's grace designed to result in our abounding in every good work.

Don't settle for less than God's best. Notice that this fruit is not a personal, private matter that is limited to you and what you get out of it. Abounding is much more profound than that. This fruit bearing is for the glory of God and the furtherance of the Gospel.

An abiding branch bearing abounding fruit—that is the goal. The ultimate abounding is spiritual reproduction, spiritual multiplication. This happens only through abiding in the Vine of Jesus.

CONNECTING

Adoration & Attitude

Ascribe to the LORD the glory due His name; worship the LORD in the splendor of holiness.

Psalm 29:2

You've had a challenging week. Family struggles and vocational frustrations have taken their toll. Even with some kick-back time on Saturday, when Saturday evening rolls around you realize that your attitude is still not right. You think about going to church tomorrow morning and conclude that with the state of your attitude, attempting to engage in adoration and worship would be hypocritical. What do you do? Do you go to church and go through the motions? Do you stay home?

What is the connection between adoration and attitude? The Bible has some answers for us. As in a number of issues we face as followers of Christ, we begin with a vitally important foundational consideration. The battle is between being God-centered and me-centered. Is my focus on God or me?

- Adoration is God-centered and Christ-focused.
- Attitude, robbed of its spiritual oversight, is me-centered and circumstance-focused.

We use the word adoration as an umbrella term that covers worship, praise and celebration. The Bible presents this activity as a vital staple in our spiritual habits. The more we engage in

15

adoration, the more we focus on our Lord. The more we focus on our Lord, the less we focus on ourselves and our circumstances.

> *Ascribe to the LORD, O clans of the peoples, ascribe to the LORD glory and strength! Ascribe to the LORD the glory due His name; bring an offering and come before him! Worship the LORD in the splendor of holiness.*[14]

When this takes place, the exhortation of Philippians 2 begins to take root in our spiritual lives.

> *Your attitude should be the same as that of Christ Jesus...*[15]

Jesus, in His incarnation, displayed an attitude that was patently God-centered.

Adoration is a major weapon in combating the attitude struggles we face. Adoration provides the spiritual oversight for the Lord to keep our attitude Christ-centered. To cease adoration until our attitude is corrected is to play into the strategy of our arch-enemy. Anything Satan can do to get us to stay home from church and to cease our daily personal adoration of the Lord will bring a sadistic smirk to his face.

Now, let's expand the importance of this adoration/attitude connection. So far, your response could easily be, "The Sunday attitude issue is not my problem. The problem is that Monday comes around, and I have to go back to the daily grind." I know all too well that you have chores and assignments and

---

[14] 1 Chronicles 16:28-29.
[15] Philippians 2:5 (NASB).

people conspiring to bring potential distraction and irritation. We all do. Our attitudes are under constant assault.

This is why we need to see adoration as far more than a Sunday activity. Actually, adoration is a spiritual weapon given to us that will help us live victoriously while in the midst of these ongoing battles. Adoration needs to be developed into a daily exercise so that it becomes a spiritual habit. Engaging in daily personal worship that centers on the Word of God and the adoration of our Lord provides the spiritual strength we need, focusing our thoughts on Jesus as we enter the "daily grind."

As you sit in traffic, as you walk down the hall to your next class, as you wait for your next appointment, as you take a two-minute break from multi-tasking, use a short intercessory prayer, a Bible verse from your memory bank or a stanza from a favorite hymn or song to center your adoration in Christ. This is the best approach to keep your attitude positive and productive.

Invest time into your daily personal worship and adoration. Go to church. Be an active participant in the worship service. Be a follower of Christ who experiences an attitude that is saturated with adoration of Christ.

Let us say, "Lord, help us to deepen our adoration so that we will be made new in the attitude of our minds" (see Ephesians 4:23).

CONNECTING

Blessings & Battles

And that all this assembly may know that the LORD saves not with sword and spear. For the battle is the LORD's, and He will give you into our hand.
1 Samuel 17:47

Blessed is the man who remains steadfast under trial, for when he has stood the test he will receive the crown of life, which God has promised to those who love Him.
James 1:12

"We deserve better. Trust in Jesus who will provide you with all that you deserve. Jesus will give you good health, a wonderful family, a great job and an overall magnificent life."

This great-sounding offer is dreadfully wrong on a number of levels. First, we do not deserve better. We deserve worse. We deserve to suffer God's holy wrath through all eternity in hell. The Gospel of Grace provides for us what we do not deserve. Second, it totally ignores the intense spiritual battle that is raging and will continue to intensify until Jesus comes again. Third, it places the material, physical and temporal above the spiritual and eternal. Finally, it could not be more unbiblical.

Here we will focus on the misguided teaching that contends that when we follow Jesus, He will increase our blessings by decreasing our battles. Again, great-sounding and pleasing to the emotions. Again, totally off-base.

Jesus says just the opposite:

"I have said these things to you, that in Me you may have peace. In the world you will have tribulation. But take heart; I have overcome the world."[16]

Jesus connects blessings with battles. These are not battles over petty issues and insignificant matters. These are the battles that come when we live with a bold courageousness as citizens of Christ's kingdom in the middle of this present evil age where Satan is alive and active.

Jesus said, "Blessed are those who are persecuted for right- eousness' sake, for theirs is the kingdom of heaven. Blessed are you when others revile you and persecute you and utter all kinds of evil against you falsely on My account. Rejoice and be glad, for your reward is great in heaven, for so they persecuted the prophets who were before you."[17]

Do you see why it is so spiritually dangerous to teach that following Jesus produces a problem-free, battle-free, stress-free life that is accompanied by financial and material prosperity? When such freedom does not happen, people walk away with despondency, concluding they tried that "Christianity thing" but it did not work. The problem is that they did not try a bibli- cal Christianity, but a cultural and false substitute.

Paul, who faced more than his share of battles for the sake of righteousness, actually views this dimension of the Christian

---

[16] John 16:33.
[17] Matthew 5:10-12.

life as a privilege to be embraced, not avoided. Writing from a prison cell, he encourages his Philippian friends to look at their lives as citizens of the Kingdom of God, remembering that they are aliens and strangers in this world. As you read the following verses, keep in mind that Paul is sitting in a prison cell. In the first century, prisons were not country clubs; they really were prisons.

> *Only let your manner of life be worthy of the gospel of Christ, so that whether I come and see you or am absent, I may hear of you that you are standing firm in one spirit, with one mind striving side by side for the faith of the gospel, and not frightened in anything by your opponents. This is a clear sign to them of their destruction, but of your salvation, and that from God. For it has been granted to you that for the sake of Christ you should not only believe in Him but also suffer for His sake, engaged in the same conflict that you saw I had and now hear that I still have.*[18]

The battles are real. So are our spiritual weapons. So is our victorious Lord whom we follow. So are the blessings that come through the battles we fight for the cause of Christ.

These battles can be ongoing and long in duration. Thankfully, our God-given grace to fight and endure is as well.

Run from the battles and you miss the blessing of the Lord. Grumble about the battles and you miss the blessing of the Lord. Stress out about the battles and you miss the blessing of the Lord.

---

[18] Philippians 1:27-30.

21

Fight the battles with the strength and weapons that the Lord provides and you will emerge from each and every one blessed, even if the ultimate victory is not fully realized until we enter heaven.

CONNECTING

Commitment & Contentment

And now I commend you to God and to the word of His grace, which is able to build you up and to give you the inheritance among all those who are sanctified.
Acts 20:32

Now there is great gain in godliness with contentment.
1 Timothy 6:6

I am a preaching pastor. I preach two different sermons nearly every Sunday. Now, without being melodramatic, I can honestly write that every Monday it would be easy for me to resign. After the all-day adrenaline rush of the day before, Monday is a challenging day. I call it my "thick" day. Whenever I tell people in my church what I have just told you, they invariably inquire as to why I do not take Monday as my day off. (I take Friday.) The answer is simple: I will not give my wife the worst day in my week. Every Monday could easily be a day of discontent.

In re-reading these few sentences, I realize that I could be construed as complaining, being negative. Believe me, I am not. I love my calling to be a pastor. I cherish the role as Bible student and Bible teacher. I consider my vocation a blessing from the Lord.

It took me quite a few years to figure it out, but I have discovered the secret of taking a day that, on the human level, would be a day of discontent and transforming it into an experience of contentment. I don't know about you, but I only take action when I become discontented with discontentment.

We can trace this discovery back to its starting point. For me, it began by asking the Lord for practical application of verses most of us have read many times:

Not that I am speaking of being in need, for I have learned in whatever situation I am to be content. I know how to be brought low, and I know how to abound. In any and every circumstance, I have learned the secret of facing plenty and hunger, abundance and need.[19]

Good days or bad days. Plenty or want. Feeling great or battling a migraine. Well-rested or running on empty. All of these possibilities are under the sovereign control of my Lord, and He informs me that it is possible to be content in all scenarios. The contentment does not come when I am able to change the "negative" to a "positive" in each equation. The contentment comes when I commit myself to His provision and His answer. With Paul, we can say, "I can do all things through Him who strengthens me" (Philippians 4:13).

Now I do not simply have challenging, thick Mondays. I have good, positive, productive, challenging, thick Mondays. My humanity still has its say every Monday morning when I wake up. But my habitual Monday commitment is to get up, shower, go to my study and dive into the day. I am still amazed at how much I can accomplish on Monday.

---

[19] Philippians 4:11-12.

But then, I shouldn't be. Commitment and contentment are connected to provide a wonderful spiritual supply of strength for each day, whatever the day may present.

Living as fallen people in this fallen world, we all face the situations and circumstances that could easily produce discontent. I am sure that you have situations in your life that could easily lead to discontent. In fact, maybe that is exactly what is happening to you right now.

I hope that you will commit yourself to His provision and His answer, thereby experiencing contentment instead. It is a marvelous benefit of God's grace.

CONNECTING

Crisis & Calm

Even though I walk through the valley of the shadow of death, I will fear no evil, for You are with me; Your rod and Your staff, they comfort me.

Psalm 23:4

You are in one of four possible states right now: in the middle of a crisis, just coming out of a crisis, between crises or just going into a crisis. There are no crisis-free zones in this fallen world. Thankfully, that will change in eternity. Heaven is a crisis-free zone.

Facing tough times is one of the toughest assignments in life. We are not the first, nor will we be the last, to face crises. Hard times abound. We will highlight two Gospel accounts of events in the lives of Jesus and His disciples to illustrate an unexpected connection between crisis and calm.

First, John 6 records an insightful account of the disciples of Jesus facing a hard time. They faced a crisis because of what Jesus was saying and teaching.

When many of His disciples heard it, they said, "This is a hard saying; who can listen to it?" After this many of His disciples turned back and no longer walked with Him.[20]

It is interesting that Jesus did not run after them, attempting to get them to stay. He didn't change His message or lower His

---

[20] John 6:60,66.

standards. He didn't accommodate to their demands or give in to what they thought He should teach. He posed one of the most probing questions you will find in the Bible as a follower of Christ. *So Jesus said to the Twelve, "Do you want to go away as well?"* (John 6:67).

As spokesman for the twelve, Peter gave a profound response: *"Lord, to whom shall we go? You have the words of eternal life, and we have believed, and have come to know, that You are the Holy One of God"* (John 6:68-69).

This answers the question, "Where do we turn in hard times, during times of crisis?" Two options present themselves: either turn away from the Lord or toward the Lord.

The second episode takes place in a boat in the middle of the Sea of Galilee. This crisis came because they followed Jesus. Yet another proof that following Christ is not a promise of a life of comfort and ease! The Gospel of Mark needs only seven verses to tell the complete story:

> *On that day, when evening had come, He said to them, "Let us go across to the other side." And leaving the crowd, they took Him with them in the boat, just as He was. And other boats were with Him. And a great windstorm arose, and the waves were breaking into the boat, so that the boat was already filling. But He was in the stern, asleep on the cushion. And they woke Him and said to Him, "Teacher, do you not care that we are perishing?" And He awoke and rebuked the wind and said to the sea, "Peace! Be still!" And the wind ceased, and there was a great calm. He said to them, "Why are you so afraid? Have you still no faith?" And they were*

filled with great fear and said to one another, "Who then is this, that even the wind and the sea obey Him?"[21]

The storm came. The disciples panicked; they were filled with fear and accused Jesus of not caring. Jesus was calm, sound asleep. As usual, Jesus unmasks the real issue. It was not that Jesus didn't care. It was that the disciples lacked faith!

The connection between crisis and calm is established by faith or the lack thereof. Lack of faith will result in some type of panic when the crisis hits. Solid faith will allow for spiritual and emotional calm when the crisis hits.

Since Jesus is Lord of all, even over the crises and the tough times, we have to assume that Christianity, somehow, should make a difference in the manner in which we act and react in the midst of the crisis. This type of faith is not a blind leap into the dark. This type of faith is not some illogical, irrational conclusion that we can only reach by putting our minds in neutral. This type of faith is the objective result of knowing Christ and believing what the Bible teaches.

In my mind I can rehearse the real life events surrounding two families. Both families were members and regular participants in the life of the local church. Both faced crisis after crisis due to ongoing serious health issues of the husband and father in the family. Both had to deal with bad news after bad news. Both had to deal with questions regarding the health care that was forthcoming. Both had to make decisions that could lead to second-guessing down the road.

---

[21] Mark 4:35-41.

As their pastor, I was with them often and was on the scene during extremely stressful times. The responses and the emotional atmosphere could not have been more different. It was like night and day. One wife was calm, controlled, thoughtful and respectful. Her conversation quickly gave evidence of her biblical foundation, a dependence on prayer and profound level of trust. The other wife was emotional, often to the point of hysterical. She quickly alienated the medical personnel tending to her husband's needs. She was critical to the point of being obnoxious. One could talk to her for a long time and her conversation was devoid of any type of spiritual reference. More than once I had to strongly and firmly tell her to be quiet and listen to what I had to say to her.

Of this I am certain: if I could see a DVD of each life in the months and years preceding the crisis, there would be a qualitative difference. One would chronicle a consistent involvement in the spiritual disciplines (e.g. prayer, Bible study, worship). The other would be almost devoid of such activity. Let me be clear, the disciplines themselves are not the answer. The answer is found in the growth of faith and the deepening of trust that the disciplines help to accomplish.

In both the above real-life examples, the crisis was an issue of faith and trust.

If the crisis arrives and our faith and trust in Christ and His sovereignty are weak and frail, you can rest assure that the responses in the middle of the crisis will be driven more by the old nature than the new nature.

This calm is available through biblical faith and trust. Any calm that will be evident in some future crisis in your life is being determined by your spiritual disciplines and activities today, tomorrow and the next day. If you wait for the crisis to arrive before you prepare for the crisis, you have waited far too long.

Jesus alone can bring calm during the crisis. Will you take Him up on His offer?

CONNECTING

Denial & Discipleship

Then Jesus told His disciples, "If anyone would come after Me, let him deny himself and take up his cross and follow Me."

Matthew 16:24

Assert yourself. Promote yourself. Esteem yourself. Our culture promotes the notion that self-centeredness is good and positive. Thus, my own fulfillment is the ultimate goal in life. Therefore, anything that stands in the way of this goal needs to be avoided and, if necessary, beaten away. Clearly, the overwhelming majority of hyphenated words in the dictionary that begin with "self" are in the "self is always good" category.

When this attitude is imported into the life of the follower of Christ, it produces a discipleship in which Jesus is expected to work and act as a bellhop. His job is to help the person find self-fulfillment. This reduces Jesus to a personal attendant to tend to our wants and meet our desires. It is, in essence, self-discipleship. A pseudo-Christianity, a nominal Christianity is the sad result.

The Bible presents the opposite as the connection with discipleship.

> *Then Jesus told His disciples, "If anyone would come after me, let Him deny himself and take up his cross and follow me. For whoever would save his life will lose it, but whoever*

loses his life for My sake will find it."[22]

The Bible promotes self-denial (which the world views as a phobia) and states that "self" is the problem, not the solution. "Self" is the enemy, not the friend. Sin has seen to that. Self-assertion is the very essence of sin.

When we admit that our direction is the wrong way and begin following Jesus as He leads, discipleship is underway.

When we understand that our mind is corrupted by the fall and begin to seek the Lord's wisdom through the Bible, discipleship is underway.

When we find ourselves looking less and less to ourselves and more and more to Jesus, discipleship is underway.

The connection between denial and discipleship is for our good. It rescues us from our worst enemy—ourselves. For the disciple of Christ, the closer we are following Him, the better it is for us. When we are promoting self, we are going the wrong way. When we are following Jesus, we are going the right way.

Let me state this even more strongly. When we are promoting self and going the wrong way, we are denying Christ. We are becoming a non-disciple. When we are following Jesus, we are denying ourselves and becoming a disciple.

Jesus minces no words to any who claim to know Him, but in reality are denying Him.

"So everyone who acknowledges Me before men, I also will acknowledge before My Father who is in heaven, but whoever

---

[22] Matthew 16:24-25.

denies Me before men, I also will deny before My Father who is in heaven."[23]

Discipleship is not a spectator sport. It is not a once-in-a-while endeavor. That is not an option. If you are taking this discipleship matter seriously, great. Keep following closely behind Jesus where you can hear His voice and stay in the center of God's will for you. This is where you will discover the full and abundant life provided by Jesus to His disciples!

---

[23] Matthew 10:32-33.

CONNECTING

Dependence & Discipleship

Jesus said, "I am the vine; you are the branches. Whoever abides in Me and I in him, he it is that bears much fruit, for apart from Me you can do nothing."
John 15:5

Jesus said, "If you abide in My word, you are truly My disciples."
John 8:31

This independence streak in us is downright dangerous. All personal, cultural and societal problems are getting worse, not better. Families are being torn apart, addictions are on the increase, the work ethic is all but disappearing. And the more we educate, the less we act with basic common sense. The more we live through our own resources, the more dysfunction we experience.

In the secularization of life, declaring independence from God is considered a positive development. It, we are told, is a sign of enlightenment and a necessary throwing off of the constraints of outdated religious oppression. If this were not bad enough, this very mindset is infiltrating the evangelical church.

The self-help movement, with a thin veneer of religion, promotes a daily life where the Lord and His Word are conspicuously absent. When a need arises, help is sought from any source that assists the person to remain in control and live independently.

However, independence and discipleship are antonyms, opposites. A disciple is a disciplined follower. A disciple of Christ, therefore, is a disciplined follower of Christ. He calls us on His terms, and it is for our good. This independence craze is at the heart of the very first sin.

Dependence and discipleship are synonyms. When Jesus says, "Follow Me," we are to go where He leads, believe what He teaches and do what He says. Let me repeat: This call upon our lives is on His terms, and it is for our good!

It is time to recover our biblical perspective and make a "declaration of dependence." Let the world call this a negative and naïve approach to life. We will call it a spiritual necessity. Here are just a few reasons for this declaration of dependence.

We lack wisdom. A disciple depends on the Lord for wisdom.

If any of you lacks wisdom, let him ask God, who gives generously to all without reproach, and it will be given him.[24]

We lack strength. A disciple depends on the Lord for strength.

But He said to me, "My grace is sufficient for you, for My power is made perfect in weakness." Therefore I will boast all the more gladly of my weaknesses, so that the power of Christ may rest upon me.[25]

We lack guidance. A disciple depends on the Lord for guidance.

---

[24] James 1:5.
[25] 2 Corinthians 12:9.

You have led in Your steadfast love the people whom You have redeemed; You have guided them by Your strength to Your holy abode.[26]

We lack rest. A disciple depends on the Lord for rest.

"Come to Me, all who labor and are heavy laden, and I will give you rest. Take My yoke upon you, and learn from Me, for I am gentle and lowly in heart, and you will find rest for your souls. For My yoke is easy, and My burden is light."[27]

Do not listen to your fallen nature. Do not listen to the enemy of our souls. Both scream at you to break your ties with the Lord, to throw off His control and His restraints. Both insinuate that God is, after all, trying to rob you of your happiness by keeping His heavy hand smothering you. These lies are very attractive to any follower of Christ who still places independence above discipleship.

Jesus couches this language of discipleship in relationship terms. As branches attached to a vine, we are to remain and abide in Him. He is the source and supply. Cut off from the vine, the branch shrivels and dies. That means that His control is based upon His care for us. His lordship leads us to true liberty. The limitations He imposes upon us are brought to bear because of His love. His management of our lives is an expression of His mercy toward us.

Confess your independence. It is a sin, pure and simple. As part of your repentance (which is change of mind and action),

---

[26] Exodus 15:13.
[27] Matthew 11:28-30.

declare your dependence upon Him. Trust His Word and His promises. As you depend on Him, He will supply you with everything you need for life and godliness.

CONNECTING

Excellence & Effectiveness

The saying is trustworthy, and I want you to insist on these things, so that those who have believed in God may be careful to devote themselves to good works. These things are excellent and profitable for people.

Titus 3:8

But I will stay in Ephesus until Pentecost, for a wide door for effective work has opened to me, and there are many adversaries.

1 Corinthians 16:8-9

Mediocrity is on the march. Challenge people to be punctual, and they will defend the mediocrity of tardiness. Challenge people to tend to the small details, and they will defend the mediocrity of sloppiness. Challenge people to memorize Scripture, and they will defend the mediocrity of laziness. Challenge people to witness by sharing the Gospel, and they will defend the mediocrity of silence.

Mediocrity is a blight on the church of Jesus Christ. When people sacrifice excellence on the altar of convenience, effectiveness quickly wanes. It is high time to reclaim these qualities from the ecclesiastical landfill and reestablish their connection.

While the English word "excellent" is used a number of times in our translations of the Bible, the best verse for teaching this principle does not use it. Instead, I would contend that it provides a great working definition:

Whatever you do, work heartily as for the Lord and not for men, knowing that from the Lord you will receive the inheritance as your reward. You are serving the Lord Christ.[28]

The attorney who introduced me to Jesus Christ was very influential in mentoring and discipling me during those early years of my Christian walk. He had a simple way of bringing the truth to bear upon my life. Bernie would say to me, "Whatever you do, do it with the idea in mind that you will first present it to Jesus before anyone else sees it."

So, we are working for the Lord. How, then, should any project or assignment be approached? Another way to ask the question: How can I be most effective? Will mediocrity make me most effective? Will doing just enough to get by lead to effectiveness? How about waiting until the last minute and then rushing toward completion?

A woman was offended that I expected people to be punctual for the worship service. She said to me, "I am a working woman and expected to be on time to work every day. I should not be expected to be to church on time." She left the church.

In a witnessing training ministry, a man concluded I was being too strict in expecting people to memorize, word for word, a Gospel presentation and Bible verses. He said if I did not cut him some slack, he would quit. I didn't. He quit.

After instituting a dress code for members of our worship teams, a young man insinuated that I was being a legalist for requiring him to wear a tie. I asked him if it would be proper

---

[28] Colossians 3:23-24.

for him to wear a bathing suit in leading worship. He, with obvious indignation, replied that of course it would be inappropriate. I asked if his dress code made him a legalist. I then informed him that if he was not willing to submit to properly established authority, his heart was such that it would be best if he was not on the worship team. This was not a legalism issue, it was a heart issue. He wanted to dress in a sloppy and inappropriate fashion.

In all three cases, mediocrity was being challenged, and people simply did not like it. The "I will do what I want when I want as I want" attitude may capture the spirit of this age, but it is radically contradictory to the Lord's call to excellence in the lives of His followers. Serve yourself and your desires, and you will be mediocre and ineffective.

I do not always accomplish excellence. I am not always effective. I am the first to recognize this. What I will not do is defend, rationalize and accommodate my deficiencies. I will not lower biblical standards to somehow make me feel better or give me an easy way out. As I continually challenge myself, I also challenge you to resist the spirit of this age where mediocrity seems to be the acceptable standard.

We give God our best, not to earn His favor, but to express our thanksgiving and gratitude to Him for our salvation and His continued blessings and mercies poured into our lives.

The saying is trustworthy, and I want you to insist on these things, so that those who have believed in God may be careful to devote themselves to good works. These things are excellent and profitable for people.[29]

Jesus, in His incarnation, was an example of excellence and effectiveness. I invite and challenge you to do everything as unto the Lord. After all, He is the one we are serving.

It is a good thing to devote yourself to doing what is good, with excellence, as unto the Lord!

---

[29] Titus 3:8.

CONNECTING

Exhortation & Encouragement

But exhort one another every day, as long as it is called "today," that none of you may be hardened by the deceitfulness of sin.

Hebrews 3:13

Him we proclaim, warning everyone and teaching everyone with all wisdom, that we may present everyone mature in Christ.

Colossians 1:28

Would you rather be patted on the back or reminded of shortcomings in your life? Would you rather be reminded how important you are to God or reprimanded for an attitude that the Lord finds reprehensible? The obvious answer to both questions is evidence that we like encouragement much more than exhortation. I, for one, am very glad that the Lord loves me so much that He provides both in my life on a regular basis. It is not a question of what I like, but what I need!

Working definitions help me. Working definitions differ from dictionary definitions. Taking the meaning of a word and couching it in a life application context is a working definition. For illustrative purposes, here is a working definition of wisdom: Wisdom is seeing life from God's point of view and then reordering our life accordingly.

Consider the dictionary definitions for encouragement and exhortation. The meaning of the word must drive any working definition we develop.

- Encourage: to inspire with courage, spirit, or confidence; to stimulate by assistance, approval, etc.; to promote, advance, or foster.
- Exhort: to urge, advise, or caution earnestly; admonish urgently; to give urgent advice, recommendations, or warnings.

Now, let's take a stab at working definitions for encouragement and exhortation.

- Encouragement is a spiritual ministry to help others continue trusting the Lord and continue acting in a manner consistent with being a follower of Christ.
- Exhortation is a spiritual ministry to help others recognize where they have gotten off track and aid them in getting back on track by applying biblical truth.

We need encouragement because we are fallen people living in a fallen world. Fatigue, running on empty and depleted spiritual and emotional resources are common maladies for all of us.

We need encouragement because we face circumstances beyond our control—an ornery boss, a cantankerous teacher, a complaining spouse, an ailment that won't seem to let up, the lack of a job with nothing promising on the horizon, a car that is in for repairs again, etc., etc.! How often that call, card or e-mail came at just the right time to lift our spirits and to help us refocus on Jesus! Encouragement from others is a balm, a pick-me-up. It provides positive reinforcement and stimulation to keep going.

We need exhortation because of blind spots. We either do not see or choose to ignore the spiritual attitudes and actions in our lives that need attention. Jesus employed very graphic language to teach this principle.

Why do you see the speck that is in your brother's eye, but do not notice the log that is in your own eye? Or how can you say to your brother, 'Let me take the speck out of your eye,' when there is the log in your own eye? You hypocrite, first take the log out of your own eye, and then you will see clearly to take the speck out of your brother's eye.[30]

This log and speck issue, being a blind spot, is difficult to detect by ourselves. For instance:

- In others it is impatience. In us, it is passion.
- In others it is apathy. In us, it is caution.
- In others it is gossip. In us, it is sharing a prayer request.
- In others it is complaining. In us, it is voicing our concern.

You know what I mean.

We need exhortation because of the downward pull of living in this fallen world. Left unattended, important habits and behaviors move in the wrong direction instead of the right direction.

It is like an unattended garden.When we finally get around to tending to it, what is thriving, the vegetables or the weeds? Unfortunately, the weeds are overtaking the vegetables.

---

[30] Matthew 7:3-5.

With our human tendency to coast, we begin to take important matters for granted. This includes our Lord, our spouse, our commitment to excellence and our spiritual disciplines. I suspect you can relate with me and quickly identify at least one or two areas where this drifting is taking place in your life.

Do you comprehend why both exhortation and encouragement are spiritual necessities? They must stay connected.

The primary ministry of encouragement and exhortation in our lives should always be the Bible. There are two main reasons for this.

First, the Bible, like the Lord, shows no partiality. This includes both people and subject matter. No one gets preferential treatment in the Word of God. Also, there are no subjects off limits in the Bible. The Word of God will go after our thoughts, attitudes, words, actions and behaviors. It will promote those consistent with living for the Lord (encouragement) and challenge those behaving in a manner unbecoming to the follower of Christ (exhortation). It will never pamper us or overlook anything detrimental to our walk with Christ.

Second, the Bible has the knack of doing both simultaneously. At the same time the Bible comes down heavily upon our mediocrity (doing just enough to get by), supplying the motivation for doing all things as unto the Lord.

If then you have been raised with Christ, seek the things that are above, where Christ is, seated at the right hand of God. Set your minds on things that are above, not on things that are on earth. For you have died, and your life is hidden with

Christ in God. When Christ who is your life appears, then you also will appear with Him in glory.[31]

What an encouraging paragraph! Then the apostle Paul turns immediately to exhortation.

Put to death therefore what is earthly in you...[32]

You need both. I need both. As we accept these from the Lord through His Word and His Spirit, we will be able to more effectively be involved in the lives of others, both as encouragers and exhorters.

Thankfully, the Lord graciously supplies both of these to us on a regular basis. Accept His encouragement and His exhortation as necessary for your spiritual growth and maturity. Since living for your Lord and pleasing Him are important, both will be spiritually profitable to you.

---

[31] Colossians 3:1-4.
[32] Colossians 3:5a.

CONNECTING

the Fall & the Flesh

For there is no distinction: for all have sinned and fall short of the glory of God...
Romans 3:22b-23

For those who are according to the flesh set their minds on the things of the flesh, but those who are according to the Spirit, the things of the Spirit.
Romans 8:5 (NASB)

No one relishes being told they are wrong. Even worse is being informed that they were born in depravity with a sin nature as a result of the fall of Adam and Eve into sin. This animosity only grows as the prevailing godless secularism tells kids from early on that they are basically good.

This is the appropriate time to be reminded of two interrelated truisms:

- The Bible is loaded with Good News.
- The Good News is so marvelously good because it comes on the heels of Bad News that is horrendously bad.

This chapter focuses on the horrendously bad news. That means you will be tempted to skip it. Please don't. The more profoundly you grasp the desperate condition that you were in as a person dead in trespass and sin, the more profoundly you will marvel at God's grace and become passionate about forsaking the downward pull of the flesh.

If Adam and Eve had never sinned, they would still be alive today. The Bible teaches us that the soul that sins shall surely die. The phrase—the fall of man—is used to describe what happened when Adam and Eve did sin. Externally, they fell from living in the Garden of Eden to being kicked out of it. Internally, they fell from being spiritually alive to spiritually dead. At that moment, the spirit died, leaving a vacuum for the fallen flesh to take over. Their personal relationship with God was severed. Sin separates.

This fallen flesh, not referring to the physical human body, is also described in the Bible as the sinful nature.

The deadly and dreadful effects of the fall begin to be reversed at the moment that a person is born again. In trusting Jesus Christ alone for salvation, we have recognized our sin and its seriousness, repented of that sin and received forgiveness through the shedding of the blood of Jesus on the cross. At that moment, we are made spiritually alive.

It is important that you notice that I said the effects of the fall begin to be reversed at the moment of salvation. This reversal will not be completed while still living in this fallen world. Only at the moment of physical death and entrance into heaven will it come to fruition. Consider this three-fold explanation:

- Phase 1 - From the moment of birth until the moment of salvation, you have one nature – the fallen, sinful nature.
- Phase 2 - From the moment of salvation until the moment of death, you have two natures – the fallen nature and the new nature.

- Phase 3 - From the moment of physical death, which brings you into heaven, and throughout all eternity, you have one nature – the new nature.

We are living in phase two. There is a warfare going on in our lives, between the old nature and the new nature, the flesh and the spirit. Here are some verses that clearly establish this principle:

For those who live according to the flesh set their minds on the things of the flesh, but those who live according to the Spirit set their minds on the things of the Spirit.[33]

So then, brothers, we are debtors, not to the flesh, to live according to the flesh. For if you live according to the flesh you will die, but if by the Spirit you put to death the deeds of the body, you will live.[34]

But put on the Lord Jesus Christ, and make no provision for the flesh, to gratify its desires.[35]

For the desires of the flesh are against the Spirit, and the desires of the Spirit are against the flesh, for these are opposed to each other, to keep you from doing the things you want to do.[36]

It is too bad that the old, fallen nature is not obliterated at the moment of conversion. To those who teach that the old nature is eradicated, I say, "I wish you were right!"

---

[33] Romans 8:5.
[34] Romans 8:12-13.
[35] Romans 13:14.
[36] Galatians 5:17.

Evidence of this warfare is everywhere.

- Is it easier to exercise or not exercise?
- Is it easier to eat healthy food or junk food?
- It is easier to read the Bible or to watch television?
- Is it easier to pray or talk on the phone with a friend?
- Is it easier to be thankful or to complain?
- Is it easier to stop to help someone or to just turn your head and keep going?

Only through the Lord's presence, provision and power will the new nature prevail and the sinful nature be subdued.

So I find it to be a law that when I want to do right, evil lies close at hand. For I delight in the law of God, in my inner being, but I see in my members another law waging war against the law of my mind and making me captive to the law of sin that dwells in my members. Wretched man that I am! Who will deliver me from this body of death? **Thanks be to God through Jesus Christ our Lord!**[37]

That final sentence is the practical application of the Gospel as the only means of victory in the battle. And this victory is certain!

This victory, which is ultimately perfected in our glorified state, is to be applied to our lives here and now. The Lord has made various provisions for us to utilize so that old nature, the flesh, will have less and less sway and the new nature will have greater and greater control.

---

[37] Romans 7:21-25a (emphasis added).

Jesus used Scripture in resisting Satan. He told His disciples to "watch and pray" so they do not yield to temptation. Paul revealed that armor has been provided to withstand the fiery darts of the enemy.

Employing these spiritual tools gives us the resources we need to put off the old nature and put on the new nature. Thus, we can and will find day-by-day victory over the world, the flesh and the devil, even in the midst of the fallen world.

Put to death therefore what is earthly in you: sexual immorality, impurity, passion, evil desire, and covetousness, which is idolatry. On account of these the wrath of God is coming. In these you too once walked, when you were living in them. But now you must put them all away: anger, wrath, malice, slander and obscene talk from your mouth. Do not lie to one another, seeing that you have put off the old self with its practices...put on then, as God's chosen ones, holy and beloved, compassionate hearts, kindness, humility, meekness and patience... [38]

Victory at the cross when we were justified...victory now through the Spirit as we are sanctified...victory forever in heaven when we are glorified. Jesus wins!

---

[38] Colossians 3:5-9, 12.

CONNECTING

Frailty & Following

And Gideon said to him, "Please, Lord, how can I save Israel? Behold, my clan is the weakest in Manasseh, and I am the least in my father's house."
Judges 6:15

And the LORD said to him, "But I will be with you, and you shall strike the Midianites as one man."
Judges 6:16

The blind leading the blind. The frail leading the frail. The sinful leading the sinful. The dead leading the dead. Anyway you state it, left to ourselves our path does not sound very promising. The only solution to this universal dilemma is to be made alive by trusting in Christ alone for salvation and then following as closely behind Him as possible.

Yet, far too often, as the years go by for the follower of Christ, we begin to think that we are getting stronger and stronger. This mindset tends to cause us, at least sub-consciously, to begin to rely more and more upon our own plans, resources and strength.

The Lord is not being unkind when He keeps reminding us of our weakness and frailty. He wants to convince us of our weaknesses so that we will run as fast as possible to the Source of strength. He wants to convince us of our lack of control over the events in our lives so that we run as fast as possible to the One who is in control.

Moses was weak and frail, unable in himself to do what the Lord was calling him to do. So were Joshua, Gideon, Esther, Jeremiah, Hosea, Peter, Paul…and the list could go on and on until we place our names there. Some were well aware of their frailty. Others came to that realization only when their own strength miserably failed them.

Gideon could be the poster child for those who know their own frailty. This episode is found in Judges 6-7. (Let me remind you that when you are reading anything that refers back to a verse or passage in the Bible, the best thing you can do is to put down what you are reading, get your Bible and read the passage for yourself. This chapter is written by a man; the Bible is written by God!)

When the Lord placed His call upon Gideon's life to become the leader of Israel, his response was classic:

And the LORD turned to him and said, "Go in this might of yours and save Israel from the hand of Midian; do not I send you?" And he said to him, "Please, Lord, how can I save Israel? Behold, my clan is the weakest in Manasseh, and I am the least in my father's house."[39]

Peter, on the other hand, was in the opposite camp from Gideon. He believed that he was strong, certainly stronger than the rest of the disciples. His self-confidence, which was really pride, was often on display. He was quick and vociferous in making that known:

---

[39] Judges 6:14-15.

*Simon Peter said to Him, "Lord, where are You going?"
Jesus answered him, "Where I am going you cannot follow
Me now, but you will follow afterward." Peter said to Him,
"Lord, why can I not follow You now? I will lay down my
life for You." Jesus answered, "Will you lay down your life
for Me? Truly, truly, I say to you, the rooster will not crow
till you have denied Me three times."*[40]

Realize it or not, we are frail. To all of us the Lord says,
"Come! Follow!" Two great words of invitation in the Bible.
Often they are stated explicitly. Other times one or the other is
clearly implied. Here are a few of my favorites.

*Come to Me, all who labor and are heavy laden, and I will
give you rest. Take My yoke upon you, and learn from Me,
for I am gentle and lowly in heart, and you will find rest for
your souls.*[41]

*And He said to them, "Come away by yourselves to a desolate
place and rest a while." For many were coming and going,
and they had no leisure even to eat.*[42]

*He gives power to the faint, and to him who has no might He
increases strength. Even youths shall faint and be weary,
and young men shall fall exhausted; but they who wait for
the LORD shall renew their strength; they shall mount up
with wings like eagles; they shall run and not be weary; they
shall walk and not faint.*[43]

---

[40] John 13:36-38.
[41] Matthew 11:28-29.
[42] Mark 6:31.
[43] Isaiah 40:29-31.

Perhaps the best language picture used in the Bible to validate this connection is that of the Shepherd and the sheep in John 10. Couple this with Psalm 23 and the composite picture is most inviting and reassuring.

Oil paintings of sheep grazing in a pasture are so restful and serene. In real life, sheep are weak and frail, unable to take care of themselves. They are in danger from predators; they are unable to find new pastures when needed; they have a hard time locating a new fresh water supply when the one they have been using is no longer sufficient.

We, God's people, are compared to sheep. Weak, frail, unable to take care of ourselves. Then the Shepherd comes on the scene. He encourages and exhorts us to follow. That is it. Then He takes over, caring for His weak and frail sheep.

From John 10, here is what we know about the care of the Shepherd for His sheep:

- Jesus, the Good Shepherd, knows us and calls us by name.
- Jesus, the Good Shepherd, lays down His life for His sheep.
- Jesus, the Good Shepherd, protects His sheep.

From Psalm 23, here is what we know about the care of the Shepherd for His sheep:

- Jesus makes us lie down in green pastures and leads us beside quiet waters.
- Jesus restores our soul and guides us in paths of righteousness for His name's sake.

- Jesus follows us with goodness and love and then takes
  us to dwell in His presence forever.

Admitting weakness and frailty, in the world's value system, is to be avoided at all possible costs. Even if it is true, do not say it out loud.

Admitting weakness and frailty, in the Lord's value system, is encouraged and promoted. For two reasons. First, it is true! Second, it prompts us to run as fast as possible to the Source of our strength, the Lord Jesus.

CONNECTING

Growing & Gratitude

But grow in the grace and knowledge of our Lord and Savior Jesus Christ.
2 Peter 3:18a

Let the word of Christ dwell in you richly, teaching and admonishing one another in all wisdom, singing psalms and hymns and spiritual songs, with thankfulness in your hearts to God.
Colossians 3:16

The Bible tells us much about what promotes spiritual growth and everything that stunts spiritual growth. The Word of God is clear that His way and the world's ways are opposites. So, as you read the newspaper and watch newscasts, look and listen for attitudes and themes repeated again and again. I am somewhat of a news junkie, so it is really quite easy to at least begin to compile such a list.

Irresponsibility, dishonesty, blaming others, ethical compromises, corporate greed, debilitating debt are all problems. In my estimation, complaining, negativity and grumbling may actually top the list. It is rampant to the point of epidemic.

Let me give you an example that is almost beyond comprehension. Central Wisconsin, where I live, is experiencing (at the time of writing) drought conditions as the result of eight of the last ten years producing less than average precipitation. We are about 30% below average for that period. Thankfully, eighteen of the first twenty days of June brought with them new rain. We are already nearly two inches above the normal monthly rainfall. The other day, our local newspaper ran an article about the June rains with this headline: Rainfall No Help for Current Drought!

Isn't that incredible? How can any rain not be of help, let alone a quite significant amount of rain? What is the reason for such a headline? A culture of complaining, negativity and grumbling.

Remember my assertion: Whatever is the opposite of the item on the list will promote spiritual growth. The biblical opposites of complaining, negativity and grumbling are gratitude and thankfulness.

- Complaining, negativity and grumbling = stunted spiritual growth. No, that is too kind—spiritual atrophy and backsliding.
- Gratitude and thanksgiving = spiritual growth.

The case study for people whose instinctive spiritual response was grumbling when it ought to be gratitude is found immediately following the Exodus events. If you count the miracles from the time Moses appears on the scene until the people of Israel are on the safe side of the Red Sea, you will approach two dozen. Time and time again the Lord intervened directly with supernatural displays of power that were actually visible to all of the people. You would think that they'd overflow with gratitude and thanksgiving.

Instead, at the first instance of difficulty, these people grumbled, groaned and griped. This instance developed into a habit pattern. This became habitual, their prevailing mindset. A three-week journey became a forty-year wilderness wandering, with the desert full of graves of the people. The wilderness is a great picture of spiritual atrophy and backsliding.

Gratitude is based upon the belief that God is good, sovereign and in control of all things. It is grounded in trust, not circumstances; in confidence, not emotions. Gratitude is God-centered.

Gratitude breeds contentment. Paul, writing from a prison cell, composed the book of Philippians. This short letter exudes gratitude. The concluding chapter contains one of the greatest expressions of contentment you will ever read:

> *I rejoiced in the Lord greatly that now at length you have revived your concern for me. You were indeed concerned for me, but you had no opportunity. Not that I am speaking of being in need, for I have learned in whatever situation I am to be content. I know how to be brought low, and I know how to abound. In any and every circumstance, I have learned the secret of facing plenty and hunger, abundance and need. I can do all things through Him who strengthens me.*[44]

Gratitude breeds generosity. When our focus is on the Lord and His marvelous provision of grace and goodness in our lives, we stop concentrating on ourselves and our circumstances. Rather, an outward perspective develops, with an eye to having a spiritual impact on the lives of others. This is so real that we will find it is possible to have the words "severe trial" and "overflowing joy" in the same sentence.

---

[44] Philippians 4:10-13.

We want you to know, brothers, about the grace of God that has been given among the churches of Macedonia, for in a severe test of affliction, their abundance of joy and their extreme poverty have overflowed in a wealth of generosity on their part. For they gave according to their means, as I can testify, and beyond their means.[45]

Gratitude breeds obedience. *"Give thanks in all circumstances; for this is the will of God in Christ Jesus for you"* (1 Thessalonians 5:18). Gratitude grows to more than a response; it becomes a motivation. As gratitude becomes your motivation for obedience, you will discover that following God's will is a delight, not a drudgery.

Choice #1:

Complaining, negativity and grumbling = stunted spiritual growth. No, that is too kind. Spiritual atrophy and backsliding.

Choice #2:

Gratitude & thanksgiving = spiritual growth. It is time for you to choose!

---

[45] 2 Corinthians 8:1-3a.

CONNECTING

Humiliation & Honor

And being found in human form, He humbled Himself by becoming obedient to the point of death, even death on a cross. Therefore God has highly exalted Him...
Philippians 2:8-9a

But whoever would be great among you must be your servant, and whoever would be first among you must be your slave, even as the Son of Man came not to be served but to serve, and to give His life as a ransom for many.
Matthew 20:26b-28

The connection between humiliation and honor provides a most compelling example of the extreme disparity between God's ways and man's ways.

The way to the top is up. The place of honor is in the spotlight. If an important person is coming to an expensive fundraising dinner, do everything you can to be seated at his table. Everybody knows that. It is so obvious, so self-evident, that to state it is almost to insult one's intelligence.

If you agree with the above paragraph, you are wrong.

Jesus did not only teach the contrary principle of life, He lived it out in dramatic fashion. The most important event in human history, Jesus dying on the cross, is proof positive that humiliation is the pathway to honor.

Even before His death on the cross, Jesus often had to deal with this issue. He had to because His disciple seemed to fixate on whom amongst themselves was the greatest. It is repeated over and over again, like a broken record. Among the many instances, here is perhaps the most memorable.

> *A dispute also arose among them, as to which of them was to be regarded as the greatest. And He said to them, "The kings of the Gentiles exercise lordship over them, and those in authority over them are called benefactors. But not so with you. Rather, let the greatest among you become as the youngest, and the leader as one who serves. For who is the greater, one who reclines at table or one who serves? Is it not the one who reclines at table? But I am among you as the one who serves."*[46]

Having been reared in the world and its system, they had bought into it hook, line and sinker—just like all of us have. This defective life view has only become more entrenched with the meteoric rise of the self-assertion movement where "I" am the center of the universe. "Me-ology" is the new in-vogue religion that appeals so enticingly to our self-centered propensities.

If Jesus had lived this way, we would not be saved and we would not have eternal life. He would have simply ignored our plight, our facing a dilemma we could not solve for ourselves—our sin problem. He would have remained in His seat of honor at the right hand of God where He was the center of worship, praise and adoration by entire angelic host.

But, praise God, Jesus is not like us.

You really need to read two verses again—slowly and carefully—that you read (hopefully) as you began this chapter.

---

[46] Luke 22:24-27.

And being found in human form, He humbled Himself by becoming obedient to the point of death, even death on a cross. Therefore God has highly exalted Him...[47]

Remember, the cross was not the Pharisees' idea, or the Romans' idea or Satan's idea. It was God's idea. This humiliation had been planned all along. The cross, the death, the burial were events that fit perfectly into the accomplishment of God's master plan.

Humility and humiliation are linked together. Humility is the character quality; humiliation is the life situation used by our Lord to develop humility.

Brokenness is a "humiliation experience" that the Lord designs to produce humility.

Your name being dragged through the mud by others because of your standing up for Jesus Christ and the Gospel is a "humiliation experience" that the Lord will use to produce humility.

Failure is in the same category. Proud Peter was utterly humiliated in his thrice repeated denial of Jesus. When he heard the rooster crow, he wept bitterly. All of his loudly declared good intentions of following Jesus, whatever the cost, were in a heap of ruins. He had become an abject failure. This dismal episode, prior to the crucifixion, gives way to His glorious encounter with Jesus following the resurrection. The final chapter in John's Gospel records Peter's spiritual restitution, bestowing on him significant spiritual ministry. His humiliation was the road to honor.

---

[47] Philippians 2:8-9a.

Your name being dragged through the mud and failure are only two examples from a long list of humiliating life situations the Lord uses. Suffering, unemployment and divorce are also on that list. Perhaps you have experienced, or are now experiencing, another life situation that belongs there, too.

Do not waste such experiences, difficult as they are. Respond to the Lord in a manner that you will emerge from the pain with the character quality of humility more firmly established in your life.

Few view humiliation as a positive. That is really too bad. I hope that you are one of the few, and if not, that you will join the group.

What happened immediately following the humiliation of Jesus on the cross?

Therefore God has highly exalted Him...[48]

I am not saying that God will exalt you to the highest place. That place is reserved for Jesus, and Jesus alone!

However, the Lord will honor you in a manner consistent with His truth and according to His Word. This honoring may take place in this life. Or this honoring may not come until you have received your spiritual rewards in heaven. We do best to leave all of this in the hand of our Sovereign Lord Who always does what is right.

After all, the last will be first!

---

[48] Philippians 2:9a.

CONNECTING

Inspiration & Instruction

All Scripture is inspired by God and profitable...

2 Timothy 3:16a (NASB)

Therefore whoever disregards this, disregards not man but God, who gives His Holy Spirit to you.

1 Thessalonians 4:8

"Read the instructions" is a phrase spoken by every wife to every husband, to which the husband instinctively replies, "I don't need the instructions." Some macho types might even assert that "real men don't read instructions." This phenomenon makes it even more ironic that men are usually quite quick to give instructions to others. If real men do not read instructions, I must admit that as I have aged I have become less of a man. I tend to read instructions more than in my younger days.

We all really do need instructions. We were not born knowing everything, although all of us have gone through stages when we thought we did. It is like the sixteen-year-old who was convinced that his dad did not know anything at all. When he turned twenty, he remarked how impressed he was with how much his dad had learned in the past four years.

We will proceed on the premise, therefore, that instruction in life is necessary. This leads to a consideration of no small importance. How do we find reliable and accurate instructions? On any subject, you will find a plethora of options. If you were

71

to compare various sources on a given topic, I am sure you would find differences and even contradictions.

This may be no more prevalent than in the area of religion. Thousands of religions exist, the adherents of each believing that their particular belief system is the best. They can be as different and contradictory as night and day. That is why I find it humorous when someone displays their stupidity by contending that all religions are essentially the same.

While I am not an expert on comparative religions, I can assert with confidence that biblical Christianity is unique and one-of-a-kind. It stands alone for a number of reasons. By the way, the reason I say "biblical" Christianity is because more and more groups under the umbrella of Christianity have set aside their belief in the infallibility and authority of the Bible.

So, what are some ways that biblical Christianity is unique?

- First, if you were to find the tomb of the founders of any religion in the world, you would find the bones of the founder. The tomb of the founder of Christianity, Jesus, is empty. He was raised from the dead.
- Second, every world religion teaches adherents how to work or earn their way into the favor of their god. Biblical Christianity teaches that it is impossible to earn God's favor.
- Third, every religion has some kind of book containing its teaching. Christianity also has a book, the Bible. Christianity alone has a book that was written by God Himself.

The way in which God wrote this book, employing human authors, is known as inspiration. It is the inspiration of the Bible that makes the instruction therein always true and reliable.

> *...from childhood you have been acquainted with the sacred writings, which are able to make you wise for salvation through faith in Christ Jesus. All Scripture is breathed out by God and profitable for teaching, for reproof, for correction, and for training in righteousness, that the man of God may be competent, equipped for every good work.*[49]

Breathed out by God is translated "inspired" in the NASB and the KJV. Literally, the Greek word behind the translations means "breathed out." God is the author. What God says is true, timeless, authoritative and relevant for our lives.

> *Good and upright is the LORD; therefore He instructs sinners in the way.*[50]

> *I will instruct you and teach you in the way you should go; I will counsel you with My eye upon you.*[51]

The Lord's instruction through the Bible is multifaceted, covering any and all of life's issues and situations.

The Bible makes us wise for salvation through Jesus Christ. The main message of God's instruction is how sinners who deserve hell separated from God can receive eternal life and spend eternity with God in heaven.

---

[49] 2 Timothy 3:15-17.

[50] Psalm 25:8.

[51] Psalm 32:8.

The Bible teaches, informing us of that which we do not know. In fact, we could not know it if God had not revealed it to us in the Bible.

The Bible rebukes, showing clearly where we are wrong and have gone astray. It instructs us through real life examples that God intervenes in our lives for our own good. Jonah is a prime example of rebuke. God told him to go to Ninevah. Jonah did not want to, so he went in the opposite direction, toward Joppa. During the sea voyage, Jonah went overboard and was swallowed by a great fish. Jonah was being rebuked by sitting in the stomach of a fish, with a garland of seaweed around his neck. God was instructing him through this rebuke.

The Bible corrects, presenting the importance of repenting of going our own way and getting back to God's way. Back to Jonah for a minute. If Jonah were to repent, where would he end up next? In Ninevah, of course. That is exactly what happened.

The Bible trains in righteousness, instructing us how to stay on the narrow path marked out for followers of Christ. Along with the instruction, the inspired Bible also informs us that the Lord provides the spiritual power and resources to live victorious spiritual lives.

I recently bought a new gadget, a lawn dethatcher. It came with an instruction book. Yes, I did read it the day I used the new dethatcher. Now the instructions are in a drawer in my garage. I will not open them again until the next time I use the gadget.

As I look up from my computer where I am writing this chapter, I see two Bibles sitting on my desk. When should I pick one up and read it? The next time I face a dilemma? The next time I am bored? The next time I have a few extra minutes? Sadly, that is exactly how too many followers of Christ treat the Bible.

You and I need daily, consistent, regular, disciplined time reading, studying, memorizing and meditating upon the inspired, God-breathed Bible. These instructions are not optional. They are not marginal. They are an absolute necessity for our spiritual lives. Neglect them to your spiritual detriment!

This is such an important matter that I would like you to read one of the best sections of the Bible on this topic:

The law of the LORD is perfect, reviving the soul; the testimony of the LORD is sure, making wise the simple; the precepts of the LORD are right, rejoicing the heart; the commandment of the LORD is pure, enlightening the eyes; the fear of the LORD is clean, enduring forever; the rules of the LORD are true, and righteous altogether. More to be desired are they than gold, even much fine gold; sweeter also than honey and drippings of the honeycomb. Moreover, by them is your servant warned; in keeping them there is great reward.[52]

---

[52] Psalm 19:7-11.

Men and women, this instruction manual, inspired by God Himself, is well worth reading and then following its instructions.

You will discover how to have life, life abundant and life eternal.

CONNECTING

Joy & Justification

These things I have spoken to you, that My joy may be in you, and that your joy may be full.

John 15:11

Therefore, since we have been justified by faith, we have peace with God through our Lord Jesus Christ. Through Him we have also obtained access by faith into this grace in which we stand, and we rejoice in hope of the glory of God.

Romans 5:1-2

Joy erupts when a crisis gives way to calm. Joy explodes when, after a series of cancer fighting radiation treatments, the MRI shows no trace of the tumor. Joy overflows when the airplane lands safely in spite of landing gear problems.

Whenever a problem gets solved that seemed to defy every solution, joy is a reflexive response. Phone calls are made, e-mails are sent and Facebook postings get the message out as fast as possible to as many as possible. It is an event that cannot be kept to yourself. You feel compelled to tell anyone and everyone.

In a world that seems to have increasing stresses, serious illnesses and seemingly unsolvable problems, good news is always a welcome visitor. Smiles, laughter and happiness have a way of lightening the load and refreshing the heart.

In the above examples, the stress is on a positive turn of events. This begs the question: Does joy exist only when life's circumstances are friendly and positive? Another way to phrase the same question: Is joy an emotion fueled by our current events, thereby putting us at the mercy of our circumstances?

If joy is so limited, it really becomes devalued to the level of feelings. If this is the case, we should use the word happy instead of joy to describe our reactions.

Thankfully, in the Bible, joy is much more profound than a happy feeling or a friendly emotion produced by a positive life situation. Joy is a fruit of the Spirit that grows in the lives of people who have a personal relationship with Jesus Christ.

It may sound strange to your ears at first, but joy is directly connected to justification. Pay close attention, because this biblical truth makes it possible to live with joy, even in difficult and painful life circumstances. Can we experience joy at all times in all situations? The answer is a resounding yes!

My premise is that an event on earth that causes overflowing joy in heaven should have a corresponding impact on the people having that experience.

Heaven is a perfect place. One would assume that rejoicing (the verb form of joy) is woven into the very fabric of heaven. Yet, there is an event that takes place on earth that actually increases joy in heaven. That event is the justification of a sinner.

Just so, I tell you, there will be more joy in heaven over one sinner who repents...[53]

This verse contains an excellent biblical phrase that defines justification—a "sinner who repents." This is the very essence

---

[53] Luke 15:7a.

of the Good News of the Gospel. This brings us once again to the central message of the entire Bible, the cross of Jesus Christ. This keeps the main thing the main thing.

Sinners deserve only one thing from God: eternal damnation in hell forever. Because of God's sovereign grace displayed by Christ giving up His life on the cross, we can now receive the opposite of what we deserve—eternal life in heaven forever.

This 180-degree change of direction, this U-turn, is affected by repentance. Repentance takes place when we agree with God that we are sinners, confess that sin and turn from it to trust in Jesus Christ alone for our salvation. Our sin is covered by the blood of Jesus, thereby becoming the means for the forgiveness granted by God. Someone has remarked that justification means that the Lord looks at me as "just as if I'd" never sinned.

If at the moment of your justification the joy in heaven actually increased, it is not a stretch to contend that this joy can take up residence deep down in your soul. Joy can become foundational to your walk with Christ. No circumstance, no crisis, no traumatic experience can shake your justification, so none of these should shake your joy.

Don't allow the enemy to rob you of your joy by minimizing it, making it a fickle feeling or an ever-changing emotion. Joy is a fruit of the Spirit that you bear as a branch abiding in the Vine. That means that joy grows through the supply from Jesus of everything you need for life and godliness.

Joy is a reality provided to you through your justification. It is part of the birthright that is yours as a child of God.

Paul condenses this marvelous truth into life application for each of us in a matter of a few words:

Rejoice always...for this is the will of God in Christ Jesus for you.[54]

Nehemiah validates the practicality of joy in daily living when He counsels the Israelites:

And do not be grieved, for the joy of the LORD is your strength.[55]

Jesus, while encouraging His disciples just prior to the crucifixion, offered them complete joy, even in the midst of the difficult life situations they were sure to face as His followers:

As the Father has loved Me, so have I loved you. Abide in My love. If you keep My commandments, you will abide in My love, just as I have kept my Father's commandments and abide in His love. These things I have spoken to you, that My joy may be in you, and that your joy may be full.[56]

Life in this fallen world is increasingly joyless. Life in this world as a follower of Christ should become increasingly joyful. Justification has seen to that!

---

[54] 1 Thessalonians 5:16,18b.

[55] Nehemiah 8:10b.

[56] John 15:9-11.

CONNECTING

Love & Labor

...remembering before our God and Father your work of faith and labor of love and steadfastness of hope in our Lord Jesus Christ.

1 Thessalonians 1:3

Whenever we disconnect that which the Bible connects, we can be certain that negative, even disastrous results will follow. "What God has joined together, let man not separate" are words from the lips of Jesus that have wide application. In our day and age, as love degenerates into nothing more than positive feelings and strong emotions, the very fabric of society is unraveling.

Love is something that happens to us, something we fall into (whatever that means), something that is beyond our control. One of the best snapshots of this mistaken notion of love is a change often made in wedding vows. The traditional vows end with the phrase "as long as we both shall live." With the change of a single letter, the spirit of our age shouts loudly and clearly "as long as we both shall love."

As a pastor who engages in his share of marriage counseling, I am certainly not alone in hearing the following lines.

- "If we really loved each other, this would not be such hard work!"
- "The feelings are gone, so evidently my love for him is also gone."

Tucked away in the first lines of the first book Paul wrote, we have a phrase that captures our attention.

> *...remembering before our God and Father your work of faith and **labor of love** and steadfastness of hope in our Lord Jesus Christ.*[57]

Love labors! Hard work. Demonstrated through costly actions. Going the extra mile. Putting the Lord and others before yourself. We are not told the specifics of the Thessalonians' labors of love, but they would have to be visible, measurable and objective.

Love is not something I feel; it is something I have received from God, and therefore something I do.

Consider this brief catalogue of the way in which love prompts labor. This is a first and vital step in establishing the biblical view of love within those who are the recipients of God's love.

- Because love labors, you can be saved. But God shows His love for us in that while we were still sinners, Christ died for us (Romans 5:8). There was no more agonizing, grueling, exhausting work ever done than what Jesus did on the cross!
- Because love labors, we are given the ability to love. We love because He first loved us (1 John 4:19). This God-type love, known as "agape" in the Greek language, is not human or natural. It is made possible in us only because of Christ's indwelling.

---

[57] 1 Thessalonians 1:3 (emphasis added).

- Because love labors, we can develop character qualities that are evidence of Christ's working in us: Love is patient and kind; love does not envy or boast; it is not arrogant (1 Corinthians 13:4).
- Because love labors, we can exercise our freedom by serving others: For you were called to freedom, brothers. Only do not use your freedom as an opportunity for the flesh, but through love serve one another (Galatians 5:13).

The enemy of our souls and the self-centered spirit of our age are co-conspirators in this design to turn a tremendously wonderful and important spiritual truth into a fickle feeling and ever-changing emotion.

On the day that I am writing this chapter, Sue and I are celebrating our forty-first wedding anniversary. When we were first married we were not followers of Christ. We were brought up and spent the first years of our marriage operating on an emotion-based love. In just a short time, our marriage was in trouble.

In the marvelous providence of the Lord, we both came to trust Christ as Savior and Lord about two-and-a-half years after our wedding day. One of the first changes the Lord brought to our lives dealt with this love and marriage matter. We committed ourselves to rebuilding our marriage upon God's love and biblical principles.

I am convinced that if we had not come to Christ, our marriage would have been terminated by divorce. I have first-hand experience trying to build a marriage on an emotion-based love and on a Christ-centered, God-given love. What a difference! Every ounce of labor and effort we have invested in these four decades has paid rich dividends. We are best friends and relish the prospect of growing old together.

Let all that you do be done in love.[58]

What a great one sentence synopsis of the biblical connection between love and labor! This kind of work really works and is well worth the investment. And, if after an expenditure of effort in expressing love through your life, you go to bed tired, remember that it is a "good" tired.

---

[58] 1 Corinthians 16:14.

CONNECTING

Meditating & the Mind

Blessed is the man who walks not in the counsel of the wicked, nor stands in the way of sinners, nor sits in the seat of scoffers; but his delight is in the law of the LORD, and on His law he meditates day and night.

Psalm 1:1-2

Set your minds on things that are above, not on things that are on earth.

Colossians 3:2

Since we have made a god of education and have placed a premium on degrees, the idea that the human mind is fallen and depraved has almost slipped into oblivion.

In 1909, only 6% of Americans were high school graduates and the total number of murders in our entire country was 225. One hundred years later, 70% were high school graduates and the total number of murders in the United States was around 17,000. In 1909, the U.S. population was 90 million. In 2009, it had grown to 305 million. In order to make a proper comparison, when adjusted for population, the comparison is 788 and 17,000 murders. High school graduates increased tenfold while murders skyrocketed twenty-two fold.

The mind needs more than facts and information and education.

Trusting in Christ alone for salvation has the ultimate benefit of living forever with God in heaven. However, there are also many vitally important "here and now" benefits, and living for the Lord in this life is an adventure in appreciating and enjoying those benefits.

One of the most intriguing benefits is that at the moment of conversion, we were given the mind of Christ.

But we have the mind of Christ.[59]

Remember the old commercial stating, "The mind is a terrible thing to waste?" We can now go one better: "The mind of Christ is a terrible thing to waste."

To fully develop this gift of God's grace, we need to establish the connection between meditating and the mind. The renewing of the mind is a major factor in the transformation that the Lord seeks to accomplish in the sanctification process.

Living in this world, our minds are naturally set on physical, material and temporal matters. As a correction, Paul exhorts us to set our minds on things that are above (Colossians 3:2). This discipline does not happen quickly or easily.

This is precisely where we add meditation to the equation. Meditating is a focused concentration on the Word of God. It is a significant investment of time when every minute can be used by the Lord for your spiritual gain.

In a small volume by Puritan Thomas Watson, *Heaven Taken By Storm*, there is an excellent chapter on meditation. What follows is distilled from this chapter.

Here is a working definition of meditation: It is a holy exercise of the mind whereby we bring the truths of God to

---

[59] 1 Corinthians 2:16b.

remembrance, and seriously ponder them and apply them to ourselves.

Three vital considerations must be at the very core of meditation:

- Meditation is God-centered, Christ-centered and Bible-centered.
- Meditation necessitates that we retire alone, locking ourselves off from distractions and interruptions.
- Meditation is work that cannot be done in a crowd.
- Meditation is serious thinking about God. It is not a few transient thoughts that are quickly gone. Rather, it requires a fixing and staying of the mind upon heavenly objects.

Psalm 119, one of the greatest expositions regarding the Word of God in the Word of God, is a veritable encyclopedia on the importance of meditating as it pertains to the renewing of the mind:

- I will meditate on Your precepts and fix my eyes on Your ways (v. 15).
- Even though princes sit plotting against me, Your servant will meditate on Your statutes (v. 23).
- Make me understand the way of Your precepts, and I will meditate on Your wondrous works (v. 27).
- I will lift up my hands toward Your commandments, which I love, and I will meditate on Your statutes (v. 48).
- Let the insolent be put to shame, because they have wronged me with falsehood; as for me, I will meditate on Your precepts (v. 78).

- Oh how I love Your law! It is my meditation all the day (v. 97).
- I have more understanding than all my teachers, for Your testimonies are my meditation (v. 99).
- My eyes are awake before the watches of the night, that I may meditate on Your promise (v. 148).

Biblical and spiritual education through the knowledge of the Word of God is an essential that is quickly slipping away. As it goes, we can expect the continued growth of immoral, unethical and irresponsible behavior.

I can already hear some reactions. I'm too busy! Often I don't understand what I read. How can meditating on a book written thousands of years ago be of any benefit today?

Those "excuses" do not need to be answered by me or anyone else. Rather, you need to abandon them and change your perspective and attitude. If you are not meditating on the Word of God, the problem is not with the Bible, the problem is with you!

"A guaranteed return on your investment." Hear that promise from a financial planner and your response will be skeptical. The Lord makes just such a promise. Meditate on His Word and you will discover treasures far more valuable than silver and gold.

For as the rain and the snow come down from heaven and do not return there but water the earth, making it bring forth and sprout, giving seed to the sower and bread to the eater, so shall My Word be that goes out from My mouth; it shall not return to Me empty, but it shall accomplish that which I purpose, and shall succeed in the thing for which I sent it.[60]

The law of the LORD is perfect, reviving the soul;
the testimony of the LORD is sure, making wise the simple;
the precepts of the LORD are right, rejoicing the heart; the commandment of the LORD is pure, enlightening the eyes; the fear of the LORD is clean, enduring forever; the rules of the LORD are true, and righteous altogether. More to be desired are they than gold, even much fine gold; sweeter also than honey and drippings of the honeycomb. Moreover, by them is Your servant warned; in keeping them there is great reward.[61]

Set your mind upon Christ through meditating on the Word of God. Renewal of your mind is waiting to happen.

---

[60] Isaiah 55:10-11.

[61] Psalm 19:7-11.

CONNECTING

Needs & No

His divine power has granted to us all things that pertain to life and godliness, through the knowledge of Him who called us to His own glory and excellence.
2 Peter 1:3

For the grace of God has appeared, bringing salvation for all people, training us to renounce ungodliness and worldly passions, and to live self-controlled, upright, and godly lives in the present age...
Titus 2:11-12

Using mild language, I would say we dislike the word NO. Using strong language, I assert that we hate it. We can trace this aversion to a simple, two letter word right back to the Garden of Eden and the fall of the human race into sin.

In His instructions to Adam and Eve, God used one NO, a single limitation to the almost infinite YES included for their choices and behavior.

Along with this one NO, the Lord gave a clear explanation of the results if they chose to disregard the NO. If they disobeyed the NO, death would result. This serious consequence notwithstanding, they both chose to disobey. They both said NO to God's NO!

God had provided everything they needed. Yet in short order the enemy of our souls showed up to rile Adam and Eve about the "restrictive" NO of the Lord. What a master of deception. Of course, we must remember that Satan's fall, as recorded in Isaiah 14:12-15, reminds us that his saying NO to

God was central in that episode as well. Five times Satan uses the phrase "I will" as he lays out his plans. Every time he says, "I will" to his own way, he is saying, "I won't" to God's way.

Peter tells us in the verse at the heading of this chapter that God says YES to everything we need for life and godliness. Let me insert here an important principle of Bible interpretation. When the Bible makes an unequivocal statement, the opposite of that statement is also true. Applied here, we learn that if God promises to give everything we need for life and godliness, it is also true that God makes no promise to give us that which is not a necessity for life and godliness.

Is health necessary for life and godliness? Is wealth necessary for life and godliness? Is patience necessary for life and godliness? Is dependence on Him necessary for life and godliness? The answer to the first two questions is NO. The answer to the final two questions is YES.

To the fallen nature, NO is a dirty word. For the follower of Christ, NO needs to become a positive word. The YES and the NO from God are both essentials for our Christian growth and for our life of contentment.

One of our greatest needs in life is the word NO. We react against this assertion because we confuse needs with wants.

Until this confusion is remedied biblically, we will live on a spiritual roller coaster. Our view of God is negatively affected. Our commitment to the Word of God is negatively affected. Our contentment with life is negatively affected.

"What do I need?" is an altogether different question than "What do I want?"

The reason that there is a YES and a NO can be linked to right and wrong, truth and error, helpful and harmful, God's way and man's way.

Right from the start, we need the word NO. Without the word NO from parents, toddlers would touch hot stoves and play in busy streets. Without the word NO, school children would talk while they should be listening and extending recess to hours rather than minutes. Without the word NO, teenagers would stay out until the wee hours of the morning and play with one of their many electronic gadgets to the exclusion of doing their homework. Without the word NO, adults over-spend, becoming enslaved to debt. Without the word NO, adults eat too much and engage in listening to negative reports.

One vitally important result of God's grace is to teach us to say NO! to ungodliness and worldly passions. Notice that Paul told Titus that we need to learn to say NO!

This is yet another illustration of how Satan, the master counterfeiter, feeds the fallen nature in us to turn God's way on its head. God's way is to say YES to that which He has determined we need. Our way is to say NO to God's determination. With this, the spiritual wrestling between us and God is underway.

Stop wrestling with God. Stop debating with God. Stop arguing with God. He will win anyway.

In this matter, the solution is really quite simple. Accept the word NO as a necessary and positive word from the Lord in your spiritual life. Whenever God uses the word YES, it is for your protection and benefit. Whenever God uses the word NO, it is for your protection and benefit. Every DO NOT from the Lord to us is an expression of His care and His love.

The word NO is one of our greatest spiritual needs.

"Lord, do not stop saying NO!"

CONNECTING

Peace & Potential

O LORD, You will ordain peace for us, for You have indeed done for us all our works.

Isaiah 26:12

Do you want to live up to your potential? Do you really want to make an impact? Do you desire to accomplish great things for the Lord? I cannot imagine a single person reading these words answering any of these questions in the negative.

Now, let's change the first few words in each question. Are you living up to your potential? Are you making an impact? Are you accomplishing great things for the Lord? Sadly, many would quietly answer these questions with a "no."

Following the Lord should result in us living up to our God-given potential. Numerous examples of this are found in the Bible. The parable of the talents teaches us to use what the Lord has given us to accomplish His purposes. The parable of the sower teaches that those who are truly converted will produce a crop as much as a hundredfold of that which was planted.

We could make a list of a number of weapons that the enemy uses to render us ineffective and cause us to miss our potential. One very common and very powerful weapon is worry, fear, anxiety. All three words really highlight the same spiritual malady. One thing is for sure: worry will stand in the way of our living up to our God-given potential.

As with any weapon used by the enemy, our Lord provides the corresponding spiritual armament that we have at our disposal to bring victory. In this battle, peace is the Lord's powerful weapon.

With this spiritual battle in mind, read slowly and carefully these familiar words from Philippians 4:

> *Do not be anxious about anything, but in everything by prayer and supplication with thanksgiving let your requests be made known to God. And the peace of God, which surpasses all understanding, will guard your hearts and your minds in Christ Jesus.*[62]

The peace of God guards our hearts and minds in Christ Jesus. In these verses, what does that guard keep out of our hearts and minds? Anxiety, worry, fear. The Message, in its paraphrase reads, "Do not worry or fret."

Worry and anxiety rob us of peace. When peace is absent, we will not reach our potential. Worry drains, distracts and discourages. It results in spiritual, emotional and physical fatigue. Yet, worry is an epidemic among Christians. It is almost as if their motto could be summarized: "Why pray when I can worry!?" Training seminars, workshops and continuing education cannot aid in reaching our potential if worry and anxiety are robbing us of the Lord's peace.

---

[62] Philippians 4:6-7.

Worry focuses on the past which we cannot change. Worry focuses on the future which we cannot control. With this draining focus on the past and future, we will always miss reaching the potential offered by the present. Peace, one of the fruits of the Spirit, allows us to take the opportunities presented in the "right now" of life and invest our energies and talents in living for the glory of the Lord. This is a good time to be reminded of the distinctiveness of the God-supplied peace:

Great peace have those who love Your law; nothing can make them stumble.[63]

You keep him in perfect peace whose mind is stayed on You, because he trusts in You.[64]

Peace I leave with you; My peace I give to you. Not as the world gives do I give to you. Let not your hearts be troubled, neither let them be afraid.[65]

May the God of hope fill you with all joy and peace in believing, so that by the power of the Holy Spirit you may abound in hope.[66]

The antidote to worry is not more worry. If you worry more you will only end up with more worry.

Rather, simply based upon the four verses presented above, take the bull by the horns. Resist the enemy who is using every weapon at his disposal to rob you of your peace and potential.

---

[63] Psalm 119:165.

[64] Isaiah 26:3.

[65] John 14:27.

[66] Romans 15:13.

Fight back with the sufficient resources that the Lord provides. Here is the list:

- Daily, regular, consistent attention to Bible reading and study.
- Trusting the Lord to make your mind steadfast, turning from a mind controlled by feelings and emotions.
- Simply receiving what Jesus is already holding out to you. You cannot grab hold of this gift of peace if your hands are clinging to worry.

May you begin to experience the reality of one of the great promises that the Lord has made:

My people will abide in a peaceful habitation, in secure dwellings, and in quiet resting places.[67]

---

[67] Isaiah 32:18.

CONNECTING

Perseverance & Patience

...walk in a manner worthy of the Lord, fully pleasing to Him, bearing fruit in every good work and increasing in the knowledge of God. May you be strengthened with all power, according to His glorious might, for all endurance and patience with joy, giving thanks to the Father, who has qualified you to share in the inheritance of the saints in light.

Colossians 1:10-12

I want it. I want it my way. I want it my way right now. This is the language of the self-centered, self-absorbed person. Instant gratification and an entitlement mentality provide the fuel that result in people crashing their lives against the wall of immovable spiritual /moral/ethical laws.

For instance, the mortgage crisis that began in 2007 was due to "I want it now!" malaise. People should not have borrowed and banks should not have loaned. People wanted the home—NOW. The bank wanted the profit—NOW. Examples could be multiplied over and over again illustrating this dangerous lifestyle. This mindset is behind the predominance of teenage sexual involvement, the increasing divorce rate and the ever growing national debt.

Two essential qualities of mature, sane living disappear when "I want it now!" becomes our life verse. These characteristics are directly linked to the spiritual maturity that the Lord seeks to build into His followers. And while each is valuable on its own, the Bible connects them together. You could say

that we can't have one without the other. They are perseverance and patience.

> *Therefore, since we are surrounded by so great a cloud of
> witnesses, let us also lay aside every weight, and sin which
> clings so closely, and let us run with endurance the race that
> is set before us...*[68]

> *...walk in a manner worthy of the Lord, fully pleasing to
> Him, bearing fruit in every good work and increasing in the
> knowledge of God. May you be strengthened with all power,
> according to His glorious might, for all endurance and pa-
> tience with joy...*[69]

Perseverance means that you are committed to pursue
biblical goals using biblical principles along the way. It means
that short cuts and questionable practices are out of bounds.
The ethic of hard work, stick-to-itiveness and endurance
develop as perseverance builds.

Patience means that you will accept the Lord's timing and
plan as you seek to live by biblical principles. You begin to
understand that months and years, not hours and days, provide
the timetable for living.

The one demands the other. The one develops the other.
Concentrate on building perseverance, and your patience will
quietly strengthen at the same time. Concentrate on building
patience, and your perseverance will unobtrusively strengthen
simultaneously.

---

[68] Hebrews 12:1.
[69] Colossians 1:10-11.

Starting projects, beginning new endeavors and initiating great plans is easy. Millions do it millions of times every day. Many disgruntled and disappointing lives are lived sitting on the heap of important projects begun but abandoned shortly thereafter. Abandon your "I want my way right now!" mindset before it destroys you.

By the way, the Lord is always active in our lives, working and managing events to prod us toward spiritual growth. After all, it is His agenda to conform us more and more into the image of His Son.

Count it all joy, my brothers, when you meet trials of various kinds, for you know that the testing of your faith produces steadfastness. And let steadfastness have its full effect, that you may be perfect and complete, lacking in nothing.[70]

The follower of Christ, in whom the Spirit of Christ dwells, has the power of the Spirit to develop the important spiritual character qualities of perseverance and patience. As that happens you are well on the way to discovering and doing the will of your Heavenly Father.

---

[70] James 1:2-4.

CONNECTING

Plodding & Purpose

Whatever you do, work heartily, as for the Lord and not for men, knowing that from the Lord you will receive the inheritance as your reward. You are serving the Lord Christ.

Colossians 3:23-24

But all things should be done decently and in order.

1 Corinthians 14:40

Precision, order and structure are built into the very fabric of creation. Every time we look at our watch or write the date, precision and order are on display. Seasons, migratory patterns of birds and instinctive behaviors of the animal kingdom illustrate precision and order in nature. As civilization finds ways to manage the complexity of life, expectations exist that things will not just unravel. We all drive on the same side of the road. The play has starting times so both actors and audience are there at the same time.

While fluctuations and variations will always occur, in an orderly world, routine is the norm. There is a certain safety and comfortableness in routine.

There are also negatives that come from living in a structured world. For many, routine gives way to boredom, a hum-drum sameness, a dull monotony. The routine and chores degenerate into a rut.

Much of life is plodding through the days and the weeks, doing our best at doing our best while doing the same things

103

again and again. I suspect if you presented a poll question to people that asked them to circle any words that describe their lives and "boring" was on the list, it would be circled more often than not.

I chose the word "plod" because it is uncommon. It also has a very graphic definition—to live and work with constant and monotonous perseverance; drudge.

Everything God does has a purpose. Since God is in control of everything in our lives, God has a purpose for everything in our lives. Even plodding is under the umbrella of the Lord's purpose.

So, the solution to the plodding of life is not to throw off the routine and get rid of all of the structure. That is not the solution, because it is impossible. Throw off our current routine and structure, and another will come along and take its place.

We find the solution in the arena of purpose. Our purpose is to see that nothing is without purpose. Plodding—doing the routine and the chores of life—needs to be infused with purpose grounded in God's plan for our lives.

Purpose must be differentiated from goals. First, goals are always achievable and measurable. Second, goals are always employed to achieve a purpose. Purpose, on the other hand, never changes. Therefore, we should establish a purpose for our lives by that which never changes. This takes us right to the Lord and His Word. Jesus and the Bible are unchangeable; therefore, purpose in life should be based upon Christ's lordship and the clear teaching of God's Word as we seek to live for His glory.

One key purpose of my life is to be a godly and committed husband. This purpose will never change. To help fulfill this purpose, I establish goals to help keep me on track.

Now I will use an illustration that every wife and husband will recognize immediately. Even if you are single, you can apply the intent of the illustration to some aspect of your life. The illustration is the "honey do" list.

The "honey do" list contains tasks and chores around the house that are my responsibility. Being diligent with the "honey do" list is one of my goals.

Only on rare occasions is the "honey do" list completely done. Some items are regular occurrences; others are one-time entries. Some items can wait for completion; some require immediate attention.

Now, let me be honest. One item that appears on my "honey do" list about once or twice a year is to wash the outside windows of our home. It is a rather involved chore utilizing a long extension ladder, hoses, a squeegee and copious prayers that the streaks will be kept at a minimum. If I were to make a list of the top 100 things that I want to do on a Saturday morning, washing the outside windows of our home would not be on that list.

Here is where purpose kicks in. If washing windows is an end in itself, it would be extremely easy to put off the project indefinitely. However, my purpose to be a godly and committed husband places a priority on putting my wife before me and seeking to meet her needs. With this perspective, washing windows is the godly thing to do on a Saturday morning.

Every one of us could identify many items that fit nicely into the category illustrated above. They are not fun. They are not easy. To use a word introduced earlier, they require us to plod along, doing things that could be termed drudgery. Purpose provides the driving force to do our best, even in the routine and the chores of life.

We have to take this purpose matter a bit further. It is not just doing these tasks; it is doing them with a proper and positive attitude. If I wash the windows with a surly and sour attitude, I miss the opportunity to do everything—including window washing—as unto the Lord.

God-given purpose lived out with God-given power leads to God-honoring perseverance, even when plodding is required. Now, that is practical Christianity!

CONNECTING

Prayer & Productivity

Pray without ceasing ... for this is the will of God in Christ Jesus for you.
1 Thessalonians 5:17,18b

And rising very early in the morning, while it was still dark, He departed and went out to a desolate place, and there He prayed.
Mark 1:35

Get busy! Action, action, action! Time's a wasting! I'm describing to you my personal approach to life. People who know me would tell you that I am goal oriented, a committed time manager and extremely focused. I have a "Type A" (some might say "Type AAA") personality. If you're going to beat me to the finish line, you had better hurry.

These qualities served me well as an engineer in an automobile assembly plant. They served me well as an aspiring law student. Not only did they serve me well, they were promoted and expected. By the time I heard the Gospel and received Christ when I was a senior in college, this celebrated approach to life was firmly ingrained in me. For accomplishing worldly goals and objectives, they were as valuable as gold.

One of my earliest biblical lessons taught me the 180-degree principle. Simply stated, when I have determined my pathway from my point of view, I need to do an about face to find the Lord's pathway, a 180-degree reversal.

So, if I conclude that being still will stifle productivity, the Lord tells me that being still will enhance productivity. This is where the privilege and discipline of prayer enters the picture. My assertion is really quite simple: Prayer will have a positive impact on your productivity!

Mark 1:21-34 records the events of a very busy and demanding day in the ministry of Jesus. He was on the go from morning to evening. If anyone deserved to "sleep in" the next morning, it was Jesus. Yet, Mark makes sure to tell us that Jesus arose very early in the morning, while it was still dark, in order to pray. When His disciples finally found Him, Jesus led them into the activities of another very productive day.

It is no trite saying to contend that if Jesus needed prayer in the middle of His busy schedule, how much more do we!

Prayer will be used by the Lord to direct your purposes and goals so that they become His purposes and goals. Prayer is never a means to get something that the Lord does not want you to have. Like so many other components of the Christian life, we tend to make it us-centered, rather than God-centered. Prayer is seeking after God, understanding that He is to be on the throne.

But seek first the kingdom of God and His righteousness, and all these things will be added to you.[71]

---

[71] Matthew 6:33.

The Lord uses prayer to provide us with resources that we need to be productive—wisdom, for instance, to which we don't gravitate naturally. We run to all that man has to say. We "Google" the subject on our computers. Followers of Christ, take the Lord's encouragement and exhortation to heart:

> *If any of you lacks wisdom, let him ask God, Who gives generously to all without reproach, and it will be given him. But let him ask in faith, with no doubting, for the one who doubts is like a wave of the sea that is driven and tossed by the wind. For that person must not suppose that he will receive anything from the Lord; he is a double-minded man, unstable in all his ways.*[72]

Prayer is an avenue leading to rest. Rest is a commodity we desperately need, especially when we are caught on the productivity treadmill. A prayer I often pray when ending a gathering of our witnessing training ministry that has gone late into the evening tends to bring audible chuckles: "Lord, please give us two hours rest for each hour's sleep." However, this is a serious prayer that I have found works again and again. After all, it has biblical backing. How, you ask? We rest in Jesus. We sleep in a bed. By the way, if you are up all night watching movies or playing video games, I am not asserting that the Lord is bound to answer this prayer.

> *[Jesus said,] "Come to Me, all who labor and are heavy laden, and I will give you rest."*[73]

---

[72] James 1:5-8.
[73] Matthew 11:28.

Prayer is the conduit of the flow of God's strengthening and sustaining grace in situations that drain us dry.

> *Three times I pleaded with the Lord about this, that it should leave me. But He said to me, "My grace is sufficient for you, for My power is made perfect in weakness." Therefore I will boast all the more gladly of my weaknesses.*[74]

Nearly forty years have gone by since I received Christ. I still prefer action. In fact, as I write this I am in day six of immobility following a knee surgery. My walking has been limited to where crutches can take me. Let's just say that it has been a challenge. I am officially tired of sitting!

Yet, while I still have a long way to go in learning to be still before the Lord through the discipline of prayer, I have grown to look forward to these times of spiritual rest and meditation. I am absolutely convinced of this vital connection between my prayer life and my productivity.

A quote from Augustine celebrates this connection between productivity and prayer: "Pray as though everything depended on God. Work as though everything depended on you."

Close your door. Turn off every electronic gadget that might distract or interrupt. Pray. Pray some more. Then open your door and get busy! Make this your spiritual routine and watch your productivity increase as you more and more live for the glory of God!

---

[74] 2 Corinthians 12:8-9a.

CONNECTING

Promises & Problems

Your kingdom is an everlasting kingdom, and Your dominion endures throughout all generations. The LORD is faithful in all His words and kind in all His works.

Psalm 145:13

I form light and create darkness, I make well-being and create calamity, I am the LORD, who does all these things.

Isaiah 45:7

S it down and make a list of promises that God has made in the Bible. In his book *All the Promises of the Bible*, Herbert Lockyer lists a number in excess of 8,000. If you did this with a hundred Christians, you would be hard pressed to find any "negative" promises listed. I place "negative" within quotation marks to emphasize that we use that word from our limited human point of view.

"A promise is the declaration of some benefit to be conferred." So wrote Samuel Johnson in his *A Dictionary of the English Language* published in 1750. I include this old definition because it is picked up by Herbert Lockyer in the first pages of his book referenced above. Of special note is the word "benefit." If something is of benefit to you, is it "positive" or "negative"? Therefore, lists of God's promises focus on those declarations from God that result in some benefit to us—something positive.

Before we go any further, let's have Webster chime in on the discussion with his definition: "One's pledge to another to do or not to do something specified…"

"To do or not to do something specified." Is this 'something' positive or negative? A father makes this statement to his son: "If you maintain at least a 3.0 grade point average in college, I will pay your tuition." How many promises did the father just make? Two. He promised to pay with a 3.0 or higher GPA. He promised not to pay if the GPA was 2.99 or lower. The second is not a threat; it is a promise.

While there are unconditional promises that God makes to His children, there are also conditional promises. It is important to know the distinction between the two.

Here is an unconditional promise that God has made to the person who has trusted in Christ alone for salvation:

God has said, "I will never leave you nor forsake you."[75]

Conditional promises are often stated with the "If, then," formula. As we turn to these conditional promises, I am going to rock the boat! God promised to give you problems. God promised to give you fearful plagues, long disaster and severe, lingering illnesses. Make this statement to a group of Christians and be prepared for some strong responses.

Deuteronomy 28 is an insightful chapter to establish the truth that there is a distinct connection between God's promises and our problems. The first fourteen verses of the chapter

---

[75] Hebrews 13:5b.

record promised blessings for obedience. These are the types of promises that we might typically write on a list of biblical promises. From verse fifteen until the end of the chapter, we have a very detailed and hard-hitting list of promised curses for disobedience.

To allow God to speak for Himself, I am including a representative sampling. It may make you uncomfortable (no, it will make you uncomfortable), but I encourage you to read slowly and carefully these hard-hitting verses:

But if you will not obey the voice of the LORD your God or be careful to do all His commandments and His statutes that I command you today, then all these curses shall come upon you and overtake you. Cursed shall you be in the city, and cursed shall you be in the field. The LORD will send on you curses, confusion, and frustration in all that you undertake to do, until you are destroyed and perish quickly on account of the evil of your deeds, because you have forsaken Me. The LORD will make the pestilence stick to you until He has consumed you off the land that you are entering to take possession of it. The LORD will strike you with wasting disease and with fever, inflammation and fiery heat, and with drought and with blight and with mildew. They shall pursue you until you perish. And the heavens over your head shall be bronze, and the earth under you shall be iron. The LORD will make the rain of your land powder. From heaven dust shall come down on you until you are destroyed.[76]

---

[76] Deuteronomy 28:15-16, 20-24.

If you are not careful to do all the words of this law that are written in this book, that you may fear this glorious and awesome Name, the LORD your God, then the LORD will bring on you and your offspring extraordinary afflictions, afflictions severe and lasting, and sicknesses grievous and lasting. And He will bring upon you again all the diseases of Egypt, of which you were afraid, and they shall cling to you. Every sickness also and every affliction that is not recorded in the book of this law, the LORD will bring upon you, until you are destroyed. Whereas you were as numerous as the stars of heaven, you shall be left few in number, because you did not obey the voice of the LORD your God. And as the LORD took delight in doing you good and multiplying you, so the LORD will take delight in bringing ruin upon you and destroying you. And you shall be plucked off the land that you are entering to take possession of it.[77]

I am not contending that all of our problems are the result of God's promised curses for our disobedience. However, this point of "negative" promises needs to be strongly emphasized because we live in an evangelical culture that never even considers that our problems may be the result of personal, present and willful sin in our lives.

Maybe you are wondering why it seems the Lord has not carried out all of these promised curses listed in Deuteronomy 28. He has. All of these sins, yours and mine, have been borne by Jesus in our place on the cross. Grace is in action. Forgiveness

---

[77] Deuteronomy 28:58-63.

is certain. However, there are many times when we will, and need to, bear the consequences of this forgiven sin.

After saying all of this, we now return to Samuel Johnson's definition of promise and the word "benefit." All of these consequences are for our benefit. We sin, willfully disobey and turn away from God. Now, which action of God is to our benefit?

- For Him to do nothing and let us continue down the path of spiritual disaster, ruining our lives and impacting others in our wake.
- For Him to bring problems into our lives to get us to stop, repent, make a U-turn and run back to the Lord.

God's promise and pledge is to do whatever is necessary to bring glory to Himself. If God's promises are for some benefit, it is His benefit. When God benefits, we benefit. God always works for the glory of His Name and the good of His people.

CONNECTING

Reaping & Rewards

City dwellers face a challenge as they read the picture language and parables of the Bible. So many of them are agrarian. Farming, horticulture and animals are the stuff of rural life. Reaping is one of those agrarian words. The word is used approximately 52 times in the ESV, often figuratively. Figurative language is only useful if we first understand the literal meaning.

Here is an example of the literal use of reaping:

When you reap the harvest of your land, you shall not reap your field right up to its edge, neither shall you gather the gleanings after your harvest.[78]

A farmer plants wheat seed in his field. The wheat grows and is ready to harvest. When he cuts and gathers his crop he is reaping.

Most often in the Bible, "reap" is used in a figurative or metaphorical sense. This does not in any way lessen or minimize the word. In fact, figurative language can bring vividness to ideas and truth through the mental images conjured up from the literal meaning.

---

[78] Leviticus 19:9.

The point is this: whoever sows sparingly will also reap sparingly, and whoever sows bountifully will also reap bountifully.[79]

The context of this verse is generosity in giving. A mental image of one farmer sowing one handful of wheat seed in his one-acre field and his neighbor farmer sowing 100 pounds of wheat seed in his one-acre field comes to mind. It is a short step to the image of each going out to their respective fields at harvest time.

This expanded meaning now includes the obtaining of a return or a reward. Reaping is to obtain as a result of effort.

Do not be deceived: God is not mocked for whatever one sows, that will he also reap. This scriptural truth, stated succinctly in Galatians 6:7-8, is a spiritual law that needs to find residence in our hearts and lives.

Every action of obedience is the labor of sowing. Every action of disobedience is the labor of sowing.

While we will emphasize the obedience side of the equation, don't forget the disobedience side. The question is not whether we sow or reap. We are sowing and we will reap. Joyful obedience in response to the Lordship of Christ is the motivation for sowing to please the Spirit. (See Galatians 6:8.)

He who plants and he who waters are one, and each will receive his wages according to his labor.[80]

---

[79] 2 Corinthians 9:6
[80] 1 Corinthians 3:8.

We could substitute the word reap in place of "be rewarded" and remain true to the meaning of the text.

One way to catalogue the rewards of reaping because we have labored in a manner pleasing to the Lord is by listing the mentions of crowns in the Bible. There is a crown (the Greek word diadem) reserved for Jesus. Then there are crowns (a different Greek word) awarded to faithful followers of Christ, a reward as they reap what they have sown.

We will not, and should not, attempt to usurp the crown reserved for the King of Kings. It is His and His alone! On the other hand, the life of obedience is rewarded by our Lord.

Henceforth there is laid up for me the crown of righteousness, which the Lord, the righteous judge, will award to me on that Day, and not only to me but also to all who have loved His appearing.[81]

Blessed is the man who remains steadfast under trial, for when he has stood the test he will receive the crown of life, which God has promised to those who love Him.[82]

And when the chief Shepherd appears, you will receive the unfading crown of glory.[83]

Every athlete exercises self-control in all things. They do it to receive a perishable wreath, but we an imperishable.[84]

---

[81] 2 Timothy 4:8.
[82] James 1:12.
[83] 1 Peter 5:4.
[84] 1 Corinthians 9:25.

Caution! Do not attach the worldly idea of accumulation to this wonderful spiritual truth. "The more the better. Then I can strut around in heaven and everyone will see what a great follower of Christ I was. Maybe I can figure out a way to balance four crowns on my head at the same time." If that is your attitude, you don't need to concern yourself about a multiplicity of crowns in heaven. You won't be receiving any!

The Lord has already informed us as to their usefulness in heaven. They will not go in a trophy case. They will not be a part of our heavenly attire. They will be used in our worship of the Lamb on His throne!

> *And whenever the living creatures give glory and honor and thanks to Him who is seated on the throne, who lives forever and ever, the twenty-four elders fall down before Him who is seated on the throne and worship Him who lives forever and ever. They cast their crowns before the throne, saying, "Worthy are You, our Lord and God, to receive glory and honor and power, for You created all things, and by Your will they existed and were created."*[85]

Jesus ought to be at the center of our sowing. Jesus ought to be at the center of our reaping. Jesus is at the center of our rewards. Jesus is at the center of our worship, both here on earth and in heaven. Crowns that last for eternity are to be used in worship that lasts for eternity. What a joy! What a privilege! What a prospect!

---

[85] Revelation 4:9-11.

CONNECTING

Suffering & Sanctification

More than that, we rejoice in our sufferings, knowing that suffering produces endurance, and endurance produces character, and character produces hope...

Romans 5:3-4

...according to the foreknowledge of God the Father, in the sanctification of the Spirit, for obedience to Jesus Christ and for sprinkling with His blood: May grace and peace be multiplied to you.

1 Peter 1:2

C ertain words do not belong in the same sentence. They bother our human sensibilities. Yet, the Bible combines such words again and again. Consider these examples.

- Afflicted and rejoice. *My soul will boast in the Lord, let the afflicted hear and rejoice.*[86]
- Joy and trials. *Count it all joy, my brothers, when you meet trials of various kinds...*[87]
- Blessed and persecuted. *Blessed are those who are persecuted for righteousness' sake...*[88]
- Love and enemies. *But I say to you, Love your enemies...*[89]
- Precious and death. *Precious in the sight of the LORD is the death of His saints.*[90]

---

[86] Psalm 34:2 (NIV)

[87] James 1:2.

[88] Matthew 5:10.

[89] Matthew 5:44a.

[90] Psalm 116:15.

Let me quote one more verse that makes the connection between suffering and sanctification. Before I do this, let me ask you a rhetorical question: Is it spiritually beneficial for our sanctification to develop perseverance, character and hope? Now, read slowly and carefully.

> *More than that, we rejoice in our sufferings, knowing that suffering produces endurance, and endurance produces character, and character produces hope...*[91]

To accept this connection and trust our Lord in the midst of suffering, affliction, trials, persecution and enemies, we need to bury once and for all the mistaken notion that our Lord will make our lives easy, painless and happy. This ever-increasing false teaching capitalizes on the fast-growing "me-ology" pervading the evangelical church. It is perhaps the major reason why so often the Christian and the non-Christian look and act exactly the same.

God never commands, "Be happy, because I am happy." But, He does command, "Be holy, because I am holy" (See Leviticus 19:2 and 1 Peter 1:16).

Every test that comes our way is brought into our lives by our Lord to further our sanctification and our conformity to our Lord Jesus Christ. While many verses present a variety of reasons why the Lord so tests us, a verse tucked away in Exodus might be the best overview of this doctrine:

---

[91] Romans 5:3-4.

Moses said to the people, "Do not fear, for God has come to test you, that the fear of Him may be before you, that you may not sin."[92]

This outlines a major movement in our sanctification: An increase in our fear (reverence, respect) of the Lord leads to a corresponding decrease in our personal sin.

When you keep in mind that the suffering of God's Son purchased our salvation, it will provide spiritual understanding that the suffering of God's blood-bought sons and daughters produces sanctification. The goodness, grace and mercy are mightily on display through the suffering of Jesus. The goodness, grace and mercy are also mightily on display through our suffering.

God is sovereign over all situations in our lives. Attempting to limit His sovereignty to occasions we like is to diminish God's wisdom and cheapen His love. I thank my God that I have the absolute confidence in His sovereign goodness, love and control that is exhibited in all situations in my life.

---

[92] Exodus 20:20.

CONNECTING

Thrones & Thorns

...looking to Jesus, the founder and perfecter of our faith, who for the joy that was set before Him endured the cross, despising the shame, and is seated at the right hand of the throne of God.

Hebrews 12:2

So to keep me from becoming conceited because of the surpassing greatness of the revelations, a thorn was given me in the flesh, a messenger of Satan to harass me...

2 Corinthians 12:7a

You may have seen a bicycle built for two, but you have never seen a throne built for two. It is rather ludicrous to imagine someone approaching Alexander the Great sitting on his throne and saying to him, "Alexander, move over a little so I can sit next to you on the throne." Thrones are built for a single occupant. Yet, that imaginary interchange happens in real life on a regular basis when it comes to a throne even greater than that of Alexander the Great.

How do thrones apply to the follower of Christ? When you trusted Jesus alone for your salvation, you entered into a personal and permanent relationship with Christ as your Savior and Lord. In an instant, you were made a citizen of the Kingdom of God. A kingdom has a king. In God's Kingdom, Jesus is the King. As King, He takes His rightful place on the throne of your life. Up until the moment of your salvation, you sat on the throne of your life.

If you verbally acknowledge Jesus as Lord and King yet remain on the throne of your life, your supposed salvation is really mere head knowledge. It is an empty profession. You are not truly converted.

Now, it would be great if climbing down off of the throne and recognizing Jesus as the rightful occupant was an easy, once-for-all event. As you well know, we still attempt to control our own lives.

Let's be clear: Once Jesus is on the throne, He is there to stay. You cannot dethrone Him. If you could, you would be more powerful than Him. If you are more powerful than the god you serve, I suggest you get rid of him immediately.

We, instead, try a more subtle tactic. We approach the throne and ask Jesus to move over so we can sit on the throne next to Him. We do just this when we insert answers in our prayers rather than presenting requests. We do just this when we claim a personal exemption from a clear command from our King. We do just this when we grumble and gripe. We do just this when we act like we are more important than we really are.

Here is where the thorns come into play. Those who have been around the Bible for a while will recall a certain episode upon hearing the word. It is the "thorn in the flesh" passage.

So to keep me from becoming conceited because of the surpassing greatness of the revelations, a thorn was given me in the flesh, a messenger of Satan to harass me, to keep me from becoming conceited. Three times I pleaded with the Lord about this, that it should leave me. But He said to me, "My grace is sufficient for you, for My power is made perfect in weakness." Therefore I will boast all the more gladly of my weaknesses, so that the power of Christ may rest upon me. For the sake of Christ, then, I am content with weaknesses, insults, hardships, persecutions, and calamities. For when I am weak, then I am strong.[93]

All too often the very first phrase of verse seven is overlooked and ignored. This phrase drives both the meaning and the application of this text. Paul writes, "To keep me from becoming conceited..." Whenever we get prideful and puffed up, we exalt ourselves. Whenever we exalt ourselves, we are attempting to sit on the throne with Jesus.

As Paul approaches the throne, ready to ask Jesus to move over, the Lord sticks him with a thorn. I can almost hear the reaction of some as that last sentence was read. "Satan did this. How can you assert that it was the Lord?" I agree that Satan did this. The text says exactly that. However, Satan is the secondary agent carrying out the plan of the Primary Cause—God. Satan is on a leash and God holds the leash. God is wise enough and powerful enough and sovereign enough to even use Satan to assist in carrying out His will and His plans.

Three times Paul pleads with the Lord to take away the thorn. God does not say, "I'm sorry Paul, but Satan is the one behind your thorn and there is nothing I can do about it." What God does say ranks high on the list of spiritual truths in which we need to trust and on which we need to rely. Read God's

---

[93] 2 Corinthians 12:7-10.

answer slowly and carefully: "My grace is sufficient for you, for My power is made perfect in weakness."

Here is a straightforward way to address this matter. There are two options for Paul:

- Conceited and no thorn.
- Not conceited and with the thorn.

Which option makes a person more useful in the work of the Lord?

I can only imagine that this episode went a long way in curing Paul of attempting to climb up on the throne with Jesus.

What about us? Are we contending for a co-regency, a shared throne between us and Jesus? He will have none of it. I wonder how many of the struggles, difficulties and illnesses in our lives are thorns that the Lord employs when we demand He let us sit on the throne of our lives with Him?

The thorn cured Paul of his conceit. His conceit, demolished by the thorn, made him a prime candidate for Christ's power. Thank the Lord for thorns. Thank the Lord that He is on the throne. After all, thrones are built for one.

CONNECTING

Trust & Transformation

Some trust in chariots and some in horses, but we trust in the Name of the LORD our God.

Psalm 20:7

Do not be conformed to this world, but be transformed by the renewal of your mind, that by testing you may discern what is the will of God, what is good and acceptable and perfect.

Romans 12:2

A sanctified contentment is good to have. A sanctified discontent is good to have. Both have their place. There is great contentment as I reflect on the tremendous love, care and provision of the Lord in my life during the nearly forty years I have had a personal relationship with Christ. Over that time, the Holy Spirit has accomplished significant changes in me. While I have expended effort and hard work, I know that the Lord has changed me and He gets all the credit and glory. This is what I mean by a sanctified contentment.

I also want to maintain a sanctified discontent. While much has changed and been accomplished in me, much still needs to change and much still needs to be accomplished. Paul encapsulates this idea when he expresses a confidence he desires all Christians to embrace:

*And I am sure of this, that He who began a good work in you
will bring it to completion at the day of Jesus Christ.*[94]

Three initiatives and activities of the Lord are included in
this brief verse:

- Commencement: *...that He who began a good work in you...*
- Continuation: *...will bring it...*
- Completion: *...to completion at the day of Jesus Christ.*

This sanctified discontent deals with the second stage—the
continuation. The stress is on the good work that the Lord still
needs to do in our lives. The Bible uses the word transformation, among others, to describe this important dimension of
living the life as a follower of Christ.

Now let's bring in the second word to make this connection.
I'll pose it with a question: Who or what will I trust to continue
and complete this transformation?

- Will I trust myself?
- Will I trust life circumstances?
- Will I trust Jesus?

Jesus has solved my greatest problem, one that I could
never have solved for myself. He solved my sin problem. My
sin separated me from God, leaving me spiritually dead and
headed for an eternity in hell. He paid the price and the penalty
of my sin through His death on the cross. I stopped trusting
myself and placed my trust in Jesus Christ alone for my salvation.

---

[94] Philippians 1:6.

At that moment, a radical transformation took place. Having been spiritually dead in sin, I was made spiritually alive in Christ.

Since then, Jesus has proved Himself over and over again to be an amazing transformation agent. I am so different in so many ways, in my attitudes, desires, actions and habits. Living inside of me by His Spirit, He has applied grace, discipline, mercy, correction, kindness, suffering and a host of other spiritual activities as this transformation continues.

While trust is an act of faith, trust also operates with a kind of spiritual logic. If I trusted Christ for my salvation and He provided it and if I trusted Christ to work in my life and He has done it for these forty years, it makes perfect sense to continue to trust His continued work. I would be foolish to try to do it myself or to rely on the fickle, ever-changing nature of life's circumstances.

I have written in the first person. Everyone who has a living, vital relationship with Christ could write a similar account.

I cannot leave this trust/transformation connection without mentioning a future promise that the Bible has made to us. These human bodies, likened in God's Word to clay pots, are feeble and frail, and they will one day wear out. Clay, much used in biblical times, was quite strong and durable when it was new. Its usefulness has been well documented. As clay aged, it was still very useful, but would crack and break more easily. With age it became more brittle. Sound familiar?

Read and rejoice at what God promises to you as a future transformation:

But our citizenship is in heaven, and from it we await a Savior, the Lord Jesus Christ, Who will transform our lowly body to be like His glorious body, by the power that enables Him even to subject all things to Himself.[95]

Aren't you glad that the Lord finishes what He starts?

---

[95] Philippians 3:20-21.

CONNECTING

Truth & Tradition

For I rejoiced greatly when the brothers came and testified to your truth, as indeed you are walking in the truth.

3 John 3

...thus making void the word of God by your tradition that you have handed down.

Mark 7:13a

Extreme perspectives often miss the point. Usually the extreme on one end of a matter has its crosshairs on the extreme on the other end, just waiting for the right moment to shoot. Normally, this causes each side to misunderstand and sensationalize the other side.

One wonders if the battle between the elders and the young has been around for generations, pitting those stodgy, stick-in-the-mud old people against those irresponsible, know-it-all young people. This battle of extremes has reared its ugly head in too many churches regarding music: new vs. old, contemporary vs. traditional. Now, I am not about to take up the "music wars" issue here. I am simply using it as an introduction to discuss the connection between truth and tradition.

Let me begin by saying that truth is a good thing and tradition is a good thing. Truth is always positive and good and cannot be bad. Tradition, on the other hand, while often positive and good, can become a negative.

By the way, tradition can settle in very quickly. Even the youngest appeal to tradition. Our son, Jae, was five years old. One summer Sunday night we stopped for ice cream on the way home from church. The very next Sunday night, on our way home from church, Jae asked, "Dad, are we stopping for ice cream tonight?" When I responded in the negative, Jae confidently asserted, "Dad, we always stop for ice cream on the way home from church on Sunday night."

When tradition becomes more important than truth, traditionalism reigns. Traditionalism is tradition gone awry. Have you ever noticed how the suffix "–ism" can have a negative impact on a positive word? Community becomes communism. Social becomes socialism.

Traditionalism, when it leads to ignoring, compromising or adding to God's Word is very dangerous. This danger was at the root of the animosity between Jesus and the Pharisees. Over the generations and centuries, the religious leaders engaged in all three of these dangerous activities.

Remember the formula that Jesus used in the Sermon on the Mount, Matthew 5? "You have heard that it was said to those of old, but I say to you..." In this formula, Jesus was not referring to the Old Testament Scriptures. If He was, He is then correcting the Old Testament. Rather, Jesus was correcting the traditionalism that was now more important than the truth. They had trivialized truth by making it primarily external. Whenever we neglect the heart in living out God's commands, the prevailing approach will be to add layer upon layer of rules. As layer upon layer accumulates, traditionalism invariably sets in. The truth of the Bible suffocates under the changes, subtractions and additions of man's opinions.

Christ was even more direct later in Matthew. With encounters like this one, it is not surprising that the Pharisees wanted Him eliminated! In the paragraphs above, I made the point that traditionalism ignores, compromises or adds to the Word of God. Jesus takes all three of these words, and brings them under the umbrella of an even stronger word. Each, in its own way, nullifies the Word of God.

...you have made void the word of God. You hypocrites! Well did Isaiah prophesy of you, when he said: "'This people honors Me with their lips, but their heart is far from Me; in vain do they worship Me, teaching as doctrines the commandments of men.'"[96]

Paul picks up this topic in a warning issued to the Colossian church:

See to it that no one takes you captive by philosophy and empty deceit, according to human tradition, according to the elemental spirits of the world, and not according to Christ.[97]

Truth must drive tradition, rather than tradition trumping truth. Traditions begun by necessity or preference in one generation may need to give way to new necessities and preferences of a new generation.

---

[96] Matthew 15:6b-9.
[97] Colossians 2:8.

Tradition serves us well when its focus is on biblical orthodoxy. When the priority is to maintain a strong and durable commitment to the authority and inerrancy of God's Word, which is truth, we are being well-served by tradition.

The church I serve as Senior Pastor turns 130 this year. I am grateful for the strong tradition that is woven into the fabric of her spiritual life. If I could view a DVD of her history, I know that I would find key lay leaders and pastors who were sincere, diligent and tenacious in maintaining and promoting a biblical orthodoxy.

I suspect that there are some "sacred cows" (a derogatory slang for human traditions) around the church that would create quite a ruckus if someone tried to sacrifice them. As long as these sacred cows do not challenge our commitment to biblical authority and inerrancy, I am content to let these cows graze a little here and there.

We foster the tradition of truth when we guard the good deposit.

By the Holy Spirit who dwells within us, guard the good deposit entrusted to you.[98]

We foster the tradition of truth when we keep the pattern of sound teaching.

Follow the pattern of the sound words that you have heard from me, in the faith and love that are in Christ Jesus.[99]

---

[98] 2 Timothy 1:14.

[99] 2 Timothy 1:13.

We foster the tradition of truth when we practice and teach even the least of the Lord's commandments.

Therefore whoever relaxes one of the least of these commandments and teaches others to do the same will be called least in the kingdom of heaven, but whoever does them and teaches them will be called great in the kingdom of heaven.[100]

In the time when anything old is so easily discarded as outdated and irrelevant, we need to do all we can to foster a commitment to the tradition of truth.

---

[100] Matthew 5:19.

CONNECTING

Valleys & Victory

I will open rivers on the bare heights, and fountains in the midst of the valleys. I will make the wilderness a pool of water, and the dry land springs of water.

Isaiah 41:18

The sting of death is sin, and the power of sin is the law. But thanks be to God, who gives us the victory through our Lord Jesus Christ.

1 Corinthians 15:56-57

"Victory on the mountain peaks is easy. It is a natural result of success. But if Christianity does not work in the valleys, it isn't worth having at all, is it?" This quote and question is the first line in Peg Rankin's book, *Yet Will I Trust Him.* The purpose of her book is to get the sovereignty of God out of the Scriptures and into the mainstream of our lives. That is a necessary and noble task.

In the common language used by Christians everywhere, mountain tops are positive. Great things happen there. God confronts Moses in the burning bush. God meets Moses to give him the Ten Commandments. Elijah prevails against Ahab and the prophets of Baal. Jesus is transfigured before three onlooking disciples.

That means that valleys are negative. They are places to be avoided at all costs. Only bad and painful things happen down there. Perhaps the most famous valley in the Bible is the "valley of the shadow of death" in Psalm 23. Somewhat less famous, but equally instructive is the Valley of Baca mentioned in Psalm 84.

Upon closer scrutiny, both of these valleys are places of spiritual victory. Here we are provided with yet another proof that God's ways and our ways are light years apart. We want to stay as far away from valleys as possible. The Lord takes us into the valleys to show us that victory transcends location and circumstance.

First, the valley of the shadow of death in Psalm 23. This entire Psalm celebrates the providence, provision and guidance of the Lord in the lives of His people.

Even though I walk through the valley of the shadow of death, I will fear no evil, for You are with me; Your rod and your staff, they comfort me.[101]

To our surprise, the Psalmist follows his mention of the valley of the shadow of death with phrases that sound definitely victorious and positive. No fear follows him or debilitates him, for one simple reason. The Lord's presence prohibits fear from hanging around, lurking in the shadows, and waiting for the right moment to pounce on its unsuspecting target.

The rod provides protection, the staff guidance. Together, they assure us of God's sovereign presence in a place the world would deem to be negative. For the follower of Christ, the Lord's presence is always positive. What a great portrait of spiritual victory while walking through the valley!

---

[101] Psalm 23:4.

Next we turn to Psalm 84, which contains a tremendous nugget of biblical truth, one I suspect many have never considered before.

Blessed are those whose strength is in You, in whose heart are the highways to Zion. As they go through the Valley of Baca they make it a place of springs; the early rain also covers it with pools. They go from strength to strength; each one appears before God in Zion.[102]

The Amplified Bible instructs us that the Valley of Baca is the "valley of weeping." The Message paraphrases it as the "lonesome valley." Weeping and lonesome certainly cannot be a valley of victory. Look closer before you come to that conclusion. Who are these people going through the valley? Those whose strength is in the Lord. They know that they are pilgrims only passing through this land on their way to their ultimate and eternal home in heaven.

Then, rather than the valley changing them, they change the valley. They make it a place of springs. In the middle of this valley they find themselves going from strength to strength. This is yet another marvelous portrait of spiritual victory where God's sovereign presence supersedes circumstances.

Gideon's valley experience is both instructional and inspirational. The picture of him threshing wheat in a winepress is both humorous and tragic. Normally threshing wheat took place on a hilltop to take advantage of the wind for blowing away the chaff. He was undertaking this chore down in a valley

---

[102] Psalm 84:5-7.

because he was hiding from the Midianites, the brutal enemy of Israel who were once again invading the land.

Fearful and frazzled, worried and weary, he was doing his best to finish the job when the angel of the Lord appears on the scene. Without introduction, the angel of the Lord says to Gideon, "The Lord is with you, O mighty man of valor" (Judges 6:13). Gideon had two problems with the declaration. First, he was convinced that the Lord had forsaken him and his people. Second, he felt anything but mighty at that moment. In the ensuing discussion and the events about to unfold, Gideon's valley of defeat and discouragement became the place of victory and spiritual renewal. No one was more surprised at this than Gideon! This man who believed that he was small and insignificant was used by the Lord to lead His people to an amazing and miraculous victory!!

The enemy of our souls wins a victory when we begin to believe that spiritual success and victory are tied to circumstance and location. When we believe this, we try to exert our own control over the circumstances and locations in our lives. This is always misguided.

Spiritual victory calls us to forsake the attempts to control our lives and yield ourselves, in simple trust, to the control of the sovereign God. He is sovereign, in total control, on the mountain tops and in the valleys.

CONNECTING

The Word & Worship

Sanctify them in the truth; Your word is truth.

John 17:17

Jesus declared, "God is spirit, and those who worship Him must worship in spirit and truth."

John 4:24

O n the list of privileges and joys for the follower of Christ, worship is near the top. God's glorious invitation extended to us to engage in this awesome activity should not be taken lightly. The manner in which we worship should be consistent with the teaching of His Word. We diminish this connection between the Word of God and worship to our spiritual detriment. Such a severance leads to spiritual atrophy and only stops at the dead end of idolatry. Such idolatry is easy to spot: It is the worship of self by making our feelings, our needs and our enjoyment paramount.

Jesus taught us that our Father is seeking "true worshipers who will worship the Father in spirit and truth" (John 4:23). Couple this with Jesus' claim that He is the Truth (John 14:6) and that God's Word is truth (John 17:17), and the connection is clear. Worship is bound up in Jesus, the Word...and the Bible, God's Word.

Our private, personal worship needs to be Word-centered. Reading, studying and memorizing Scripture promotes a deep encounter with the living God, provides the solid content that leads to glorifying Christ, and presents the truth used by the Holy Spirit to teach, convict and sanctify. While a hymnal and/ or devotional book can be an auxiliary tool for use in our personal worship, neither should nudge the Bible from first place to a secondary position. A closed Bible is evidence that personal, private worship has not taken place.

Our corporate, public worship needs to be Word-centered. Every component needs to be saturated with the content and truth of the Scriptures. As worshippers enter the sanctuary, they should be immediately encountered by God's Word. In churches where printed order of services are distributed in a bulletin, there should be Bible verses clearly in view for people to use to quiet their hearts in preparation for worship. In churches where screens are used, a series of Scripture slides need to be rotating for people to read in preparation. The call to worship, prayers and even the pastoral welcome should be saturated with Scripture.

How about music? Here opinions, personal tastes and feelings run rampant. No place is so fertile a ground for "me-ology" as music. One matter is for certain: All words and lyrics in the hymns and songs we sing need to be consistent with the Word of God. This covers both content and intent. If the inten-tion is to exalt human feelings and emotions, the songwriter has missed the mark, since worship exists to exalt Christ and His Name through His Word.

Finally, and most importantly, is the preaching of the Word. Simply stated, the sermon is just that—preaching the

Word. Preaching is my job. Without mincing words, this is exactly what Paul instructed Timothy to do:

> ...preach the word; be ready in season and out of season; reprove, rebuke, and exhort, with complete patience and teaching.[103]

The people do not need my opinion, a discussion of current events or a series of illustrations and stories linked together. They, and I, need an encounter with the Living God through His Word. Through His Word, He performs the spiritual surgery that might be needed in our lives.

> For the word of God is living and active, sharper than any two-edged sword, piercing to the division of soul and of spirit, of joints and of marrow, and discerning the thoughts and intentions of the heart.[104]

Carry your Bible with you to worship, both private and public. We are privileged to use the inspired inerrant Bible to exalt the perfect, sinless Savior Jesus Christ. The Lord has every right to expect, even demand, that we do it His way.

---

[103] 2 Timothy 4:2.
[104] Hebrews 4:12.

CONNECTING

Death & Deliverance

For to me to live is Christ, and to die is gain.

Philippians 1:21

Jesus said to her, "I am the resurrection and the life. Whoever believes in Me, though he die, yet shall he live, and everyone who lives and believes in Me shall never die. Do you believe this?"

John 11:25-26

This really is the final chapter. And I am not referring to this book.

There is no issue in all of life that is more in need of biblical thinking than the issue of death. This is the ultimate issue. For followers of Christ, there really should be a distinct and qualitative difference between our view of death and the view of unbelievers. Followers of Christ have the power to live well and the confidence to die well.

Have you ever noticed that the pictures and metaphors in the Bible referring to life emphasize that our physical lives upon this earth are brief and transitory.

My days are like an evening shadow; I wither away like grass.[105]

---

[105] Psalm 102:11.

As for man, his days are like grass; he flourishes like a flower of the field; for the wind passes over it, and it is gone, and its place knows it no more.[106]

Come now, you who say, "Today or tomorrow we will go into such and such a town and spend a year there and trade and make a profit"—yet you do not know what tomorrow will bring. What is your life? For you are a mist that appears for a little time and then vanishes.[107]

A shadow, grass, flowers, a mist. These images are not meant to minimize the value and importance of life. Life is sacred and a gift from God. He decides when it begins and when it ends. Being made in His image, each human life is an expression of the crown of His creation. Therefore, we should cherish life and live each day to the fullest.

Rather, these biblical pictures contrast the transitory nature of life on earth with the reality of eternity. Whether we live sixty years or eighty years or one hundred years, it is but a brief moment compared to eternity.

Not only are our lives brief and temporary, they are also lived in a fallen, sinful and defiled planet that is experiencing the vicious onslaught of Satan and his minions. So the biblical warning is clear: Don't expect too much from this world and don't expect to live here too long. That is exactly why the Bible teaches us that we are pilgrims passing through, not citizens setting up permanent residence.

---

[106] Psalm 103:15-16.

[107] James 4:13-14.

We have a saying around our house. We used it when our children were growing up and we still use it as empty nesters. When we expect too much from this world and grumble because we are not experiencing more positive circumstances, we remind one another, "Life is hard and then you die." Before you say, "Wow, what a negative view of life!" remember that this statement is sound theology.

For one who trusts in Jesus Christ alone for salvation, death is no longer a dreaded enemy. The longest chapter in Paul's writings in the New Testament is 1 Corinthians 15. (I know that Paul did not write in chapters and that they were added later.) I make this comment because the entire chapter has only one subject: the resurrection. He brings his glorious presentation of the resurrection to a climax with this amazing statement:

> *When the perishable puts on the imperishable, and the mortal puts on immortality, then shall come to pass the saying that is written: "Death is swallowed up in victory." "O death, where is your victory? O death, where is your sting?" The sting of death is sin, and the power of sin is the law. But thanks be to God, who gives us the victory through our Lord Jesus Christ.[108]*

Death is not a dreaded enemy but a marvelous deliverance. When a person reports that he has been delivered from something, he usually refers to being rescued from that which is

---

[108] 1 Corinthians 15:54-57.

negative. By implication, this deliverance results in something positive.

This is certainly the case with salvation, death and the follower of Christ. The death of Christ and His resurrection assure us of the victory that makes our death our ultimate deliverance. Writing from a Roman jail cell to his brothers and sisters in Philippi, Paul penned a sentence that any one of us could easily adopt as a life verse:

For to me to live is Christ, and to die is gain.[109]

If Paul lives, great! If Paul dies, great! Talk about the ultimate win/win!

I love life. I will gladly accept each day that the Lord gives to me. I will seek to live each day to the fullest. But I am looking forward to my death, because at that moment I will experience the ultimate deliverance.

Our God in His Bible often places words in sentences that we do not think belong together. To us they seem contradictory, opposites, maybe even some kind of a mistake. Here are a few examples:

- Rejoice…suffering.[110]
- Extreme poverty…overflowing generosity.[111]
- Love…enemies.[112]

---

[109] Philippians 1:21.

[110] Romans 5:3.

[111] 2 Corinthians 8:2.

[112] Matthew 5:44.

- Blessed...persecution.[113]
- Content...calamities.[114]

It is because the Lord connects death and deliverance that the Bible links two words together at which many would scoff and ridicule. But for you and me, as believers in the Lord Jesus Christ, they pronounce a most glorious benediction. This sentence states a truth to which we cling with absolute confidence and the surest hope:

Precious in the sight of the LORD is the death of His saints.[115]

You will never die! Do you believe this? You will be delivered into His glorious presence to live for ever and ever and ever and ever!!

Now to Him who is able to keep you from stumbling and to present you blameless before the presence of His glory with great joy, to the only God, our Savior, through Jesus Christ our Lord, be glory, majesty, dominion, and authority, before all time and now and forever. Amen.[116]

---

[113] Matthew 5:11.

[114] 2 Corinthians 12:10.

[115] Psalm 116:15 (emphasis added).

[116] Jude 1:24-25.